GW00707404

AN ORGANIC GARDENER'S EXPERIENCE

AN ORGANIC GARDENER'S EXPERIENCE

Philip Clarke

The Book Guild Ltd
Sussex, England

First published in Great Britain in 2002 by
The Book Guild Ltd
25 High Street
Lewes, East Sussex
BN7 2LU

Typesetting in Times by
IML Typographers, Birkenhead, Merseyside

Printed in Great Britain by
Bookcraft (Bath) Ltd, Avon

A catalogue record for this book is available from
The British Library.

ISBN 1 85776 594 X

*Dedicated to the Rev Mother Flora,
CAH, Ditchingham, and to my mother,
who both encouraged me to garden*

CONTENTS

FOREWORD

Organic gardening may be the height of fashion nowadays, but it was not always so. You don't have to look back many years to find organic proponents being ridiculed for not taking advantage of chemical fertilisers, or the latest sprays. Those of us promoting organic gardening in those less enlightened times were seen as Luddites – the muck and mystery brigade!

Geoff Hamilton was the first popular gardening commentator to declare himself an organic gardener. It was a slow conversion, based on experiments he carried out at Barnsdale, but once convinced, he became an enthusiastic and committed convert. Where he led, others followed, and hardly any major gardening personality advocates the chemical approach these days.

However, long before it became fashionable, there were a few gardeners who were prepared to challenge the chemical orthodoxy. Most famous of all as Lawrence Hills, my own mentor, who founded the Henry Doubleday Research Association in 1954. Taking traditional gardening wisdom and combining it with modern scientific discoveries, he laid the foundations of organic gardening as it is practised today.

Reading Philip Clarke's absorbing little book about his own experience as an organic gardener, I am reminded of Hills' classic *Grow Your Own Fruit and Vegetables*, which was full of down-to-earth gardening tips and information, based on a lifetime of practice coupled with keen observation.

If you are to be a successful gardener, there is nothing to beat years of experience, but the next best thing is to tap into knowledge of others. It is clear that Philip has this in spades, if you will forgive the pun. I have no doubt that this book will make fascinating reading for everyone who wishes to garden more in harmony with Nature.

Alan Gear
Chief Executive, The Henry Doubleday Research Association
August 2001.

PREFACE

There has probably never been a generation before us so concerned with what we eat and drink and what is a complete and healthy diet.

We read the Bible from St Matthew in Our Lord's own words when he says, 'Do not worry about your life, what you will eat or drink or about your body, what you will wear. Is not life more than food and the body more than clothing?' (Matthew 6:25)

These words are just as important today as they were when written by St Matthew. But with one important difference: in Our Lord's time food was not artificial and was not grown to suit the grower but intended for the eater, provided by nature and untampered with. Our Lord's audience had no need to examine the food as to whether it contained artificial colouring, chemical preservatives, or vitamin B or C. It was easy to eat a balanced diet.

Our society cannot take those golden words quite so literally, but we have to consider what a wise diet is. Perhaps it contains toxic chemicals; potatoes fed too much nitrogen have been proved to contain fewer vitamins than normally grown ones.

Laurence Hills, writing in *Grow Your Own Fruit and Vegetables*, goes to some length in his experiment in 1960 with the Henry Doubleday Research Association, when 28 experimenters each sampled four plates of Majestic potatoes. Sample A was grown on comfrey, B grown on farmyard manure, C grown with compost and D grown with chemical fertilizer by a local farmer.

The result, not surprisingly, showed the majority putting the chemically grown potatoes last, with a majority preferring the comfrey-produced potatoes, showing that the proof of the pudding is not only in the eating but in the growing!

We are still awaiting the results of tests which can compare the nutritional value between organically grown vegetables and those grown with chemicals. According to information from Ryton gardens, it should not be too long now.

ACKNOWLEDGEMENTS

To   Bishop of Salisbury and family for allowing publication of 'Meditation' series in *Saturday Telegraph*

Mrs Hambro for photographs of garden.

Peter Beales for advice.

Heacham Lavender for their photograph.

Alan Grear for his Foreword.

Peter Harpur CAT Composing; plus illustrations.

Bowes Family, Saham Hall.

Mr and Mrs Powell, for photograph of peaches and compost bins.

Lady Decies photograph in garden.

Dr & Mrs Byatt photograph in Polytunnel

1

An Organic Gardener's Experience

It was 1969 when we decided to leave the family farm, the farm I had known since my earliest years. Disillusionment with farming was a contributing factor to abandoning the farm.

Cows had been the mainstay since my father's early death in 1944 of tuberculosis. My mother, on continuing the farm, decided to test the whole herd for tuberculosis, with the result that only 25 per cent remained from the old original herd. This would be the founding nucleus, and it was added to, becoming one of the first T.B. tested herds in the area.

Pigs had been my great interest. We started with some Essex pigs in the fifties – they are the ones with a white saddle, a white tip on the tail and two white 'socks' a few inches up the two back legs. However, with the importation of the landrace breed and the craze for lean meat, the Essex were soon not wanted. The house-wife's choice had won, and the farmer lost his name for good British husbandry with pigs so lean that they were unable to cope with British farming conditions, being of weaker constitution and poorer resistance to disease. The Danes reared them in heated houses. So farmers turned to the next best thing, namely the hybrid or cross-bred pig. This in turn was the beginning of the large breeding companies of hybrid pigs which I was not keen to join.

Before we left the farm a student from the University of East Anglia called on me. He was keen to earn some spare cash and introduced me to a selection of periodicals which might interest me. Having glanced down the list and almost decided prematurely that there was nothing suitable for me, something caught my eye, an organic gardening magazine from America, which was duly ordered and over the next year proved of great interest. What on earth was a shredder? Of course, it was quite common in America in the sixties.

On moving to a new home with a good-sized garden in a pretty little village outside Norwich, I made up my mind there and then that it would be a 100 per cent organic garden, having also joined the Henry Doubleday Research Association in 1966. It seemed good sense to eat fresh food not only straight from the garden, but also free from pesticides and chemicals. Gardening after all involves time and work and no little effort, so why not do it properly in the first place, apart from thinking of my 'living friends', the creatures who also inhabit my garden!

The first thing to strike me was that one needs a positive mind, one must think organic, never mind the easier preference.

Put away the common trend and think more about the soil and fertility, an apple with scab can still be eaten, but what are carrots wrapped up in plastic for? Surely milk straight from the cow is drinkable!

That bag of fertilizer from the farm would be dumped along with any other chemical/weedkiller.

On 3 September 1973 Mr Ted Malt enrolled me as assistant manager at Daniels Garden Centre, Norwich. He was one of the old school and insisted that all gardeners should possess a knife, a piece of string and a few pence in his pocket. There is no better way of learning about plants and plant names plus a general knowledge of the garden world than working in a garden centre. One was continually bombarded with questions on gardening and it gave me a good opportunity to recommend organic methods in preference when asked for cures of certain ailments of plants.

It is not always obvious to the younger generation that learning gardening 20 or 30 years ago was a much more difficult process than nowadays, that most gardening books of the time did not contain beautifully coloured photographs as they do now, making it quite difficult to identify plants. Descriptions were more relied upon, especially with house plants.

A banking firm purchased the garden centre. and after a short term the specialist firm Notcutts bought it and successfully expanded it as a leading centre for plants in Norwich.

2

Saham Hall

The opportunity arose to work in a private garden at Saham Hall, Saham Toney, Norfolk.

The hall and garden had become a shadow of its previous lustre. The building itself had witnessed a large fire some years previously, so the roof was missing and timbers which the firemen had saved lay scattered all over the driveway. It seemed an awful shame that such a fine house lay in ruins. The garden had been left for at least five years and become overgrown. Part of a meadow had been fenced off to provide a most interesting collection of old-fashioned roses. At one side near the farmyard was the swimming pool, all in good order.

Having been in agriculture for a large part of my life previously, it became of great interest to hear about the previous owner of this private estate. He was a London businessman named Martineau, who was a most enthusiastic breeder of Frisian cows and bought cows from the most renowned herds in the country. They were shown at all the county shows and many of them were champions. His garden produce was also grown to show standards and shown with great success.

The garden at Saham Hall is dominated by a wall surrounding the vegetable garden and greenhouses. Box hedges divided and edged the pathways in between plots, and fruit trees were grown alongside the box. Outside the walled-in garden is a small wood and walk, planted with bulbs and shrubs – *Mahonia japonica*, forsythia, *Viburnum tinus* and a lot of laurel.

The greenhouses were furnished mainly with geraniums, busy

lizzies, bread plant tradescantias, spider plants etc. There were also a few orchids, which needed repotting quite badly. Orchids were something new to me and on consulting my house-plant book I realised that osmunda fibre was required, but no longer available, so the best alternative appeared to be a mixture of peat, sand and some leaf mould, on which the orchids flowered the following spring, thankfully! The latest method since the old days appears to be bark chippings for *Cymbidiums*, though at present it does seem to be inferior to moss peat, sand and the addition of perlite; orchids also need some ground chalk and magnesium limestone. My latest experiment is to use well-matured shreddings mixed with leaf mould and sand and perlite with the addition of chalk and dolomite.

The scented early-flowering *Jasminum polyanthum* was a most useful addition to the greenhouse, like all the jasmine family, it was easy to propagate and provided a welcome spring show.

The new owners at Saham Hall, Mr and Mrs Bowes, were determined to rebuild the hall, but to a more manageable size, and occasionally I found myself fighting to save climbing roses alongside the walls from eager builders hoping to chop them off!

The main lawn has a marvellous view overlooking surrounding farm land with magnificent sunsets appearing in the evenings.

The main perennial border alongside the lawn has the garden wall as its background with *Cytisus battandieri* at one end, which makes a prominent show.

The greenhouses were of the old-fashioned type with plenty of space, and the garden wall at the back, with top and side ventilation. They contained white grapes in the middle house, with chrysanthemums at the end house and the house-plants and jasmine at the entrance. Another greenhouse in a shady part of the garden contained ferns and a *Black Hamburgh* grapevine.

One of my first jobs was rescuing the indoor chrysanthemums and selecting colours to be kept for further propagation. Names such as Audrey, Shoesmith, Beacon, or Yellows Rival, Salmon, Elizabeth Woolmon etc. were prominent and we soon worked up to 100 pots in various greenhouses. One variety flowering well into December for a Christmas show was Balcombe Perfection –

amber-bronze. All the compost was of home made mixtures. And plain coarse sand for cuttings with heat underneath.

POTTING CHRYSANTHEMUMS

First potting: 3 parts fibrous loam, 1 part well-rotted cow manure, 1 part leaf mould, ⅙ part of silver sand, or coarse sand, and a dusting of wood ashes, all passed through a coarse sieve. 3 inch clay pots were used throughout, with crocks in the bottom. Plants reared as hardy as possible without the danger of frost.

Second potting: 2 parts fibrous loam, 1 part leaf mould, ⅓ well-rotted cow manure, dusting of bone meal and wood ash, plus calcified seaweed; coarse sand (a richer mixture). Firmly potted in 5 inch (12cm) pots.

Final potting: 4 parts fibrous loam; 1 part leaf mould, ½ part well-rotted cow manure, good sprinkling of wood ash/charcoal, 5 inch (12cm) pot of bone meal plus a handful of seaweed meal. Very firmly rammed in 9–10 inches (22cm–25cm) pots.

As the plants grow, 6 inch laterals are pinched out and shoots should be pinched out at the end of June or July for later flowering.

Chrysanthemums going outside for the summer need wire supports, for tying in. They should be arranged in rows on a pathway with space between, 1 foot (30cm) apart. If plants are to remain inside they will need canes to support them, large plants needing up to three each.

As the plant roots fill the pot, they need feeding. Liquid soot water (if available) is a good starter and seaweed manure or liquid farmyard manure is a good continuation.

It is well to point out that the garden was situated next to a good stock farm and therefore two types of muck – bullock and pig – were readily available at my request. Not far away was the slaughterhouse and Mr Bowes senior arranged a quantity of liquid blood to use especially for the grapevines etc. This needed to be neutralized a bit with garden lime.

LIQUID BLOOD

If used dry it needs to be mixed in the following quantities: muratic acid 4 oz (113g), and sulphate of iron 4 oz (113g) as the blood begins to smell! Mix the later with 16 lb (7.2kg) blood; this is then a useful fertilizer very high in nitrogen.

During the wintertime large shoots took place, when meals would be eaten in a room next to the hall, the main course for lunch being celery. They would need at least three or four good hearts of celery.

GROWING CELERY

Pig manure is invaluable in the bottom of a 15 inch (40cm) trench which should never get dry. Brown paper bags act very well for blanching the stems wrapped around the plants; as the trench is filled with soil, the plants are held in position with no need of tying stems.

The most important thing to remember about celery is to make sure it is always in a large enough pot, and never to let it become pot-bound; as this will cause 'bolting' at a later date!

Celery leaf fly is often a problem, but the best cure is a light sprinkling of soot, as the crop grows before 'earthing up'. Naphthalene or mothballs can be used to deter slugs, which are always encouraged by the moist conditions. But perhaps the most reliable method, though somewhat more expensive, is to use Nemaslug from April – it needs a minimum temperature of 10°C (50°F), lasts for up to 6 weeks, and is applied with a watering can. These are naturally occurring microscopic nematodes.

Clinker (coal ash) is most effective to deter slugs if available.

Perhaps the most significant memory for me of the garden was my first looking around it, and noticing that a bed of cauliflowers were infested with cabbage root fly which had killed them all except for about two per cent. Having realized that the soil looked very poor and considering the unlimited amount of farmyard manure available, I decided that it would be interesting to remove the cauliflowers and simply rotavate a good thick mulch of fairly fresh pigs' manure straight in and simply replant some more cauliflowers in an effort to prove the superiority of farmyard manure. This followed and the result was approximately 95 per cent or more very healthy cauliflowers with no problems. Since then it has been my common practice to use farmyard manure of any sort, but always only very lightly forked in for the brassica family. Brussels sprouts in my experience very rarely get cabbage root fly.

Any queries about using fresh farmyard manure with regard to its potential as a health risk are dismissed; after a period of five months or so in the soil, all organisms are totally digested by the soil.

We had two unheated greenhouses, one for picking winter chrysanthemums and tomatoes, the other used for early potatoes and lettuce for the spring. As there was only a one-year interval between potato plantings, it was essential to use a very healthy variety, namely *Maris Peer*, a good variety often used for the canning industry.

The gamekeeper would frequently pass through the garden on his round and was not averse to a tale or two about his profession and their behaviour whilst shooting. One little tale concerned the large greenhouse built beside the garden wall and how one gentleman bet his partner that he could not land a pheasant in the middle of the greenhouse. He lost his bet, and of course, a pane of glass.

Not all gardens in which I work have been committed to organic principles, but when talking of my curriculum vitae sometimes the question came up, so my concern was that my methods of gardening remained totally organic.

On one occasion it befell me to weed the gravel paths, and I was instructed to use a powder granule of which I knew nothing, manufactured by the petrol/oil company Shell. Having proceeded as instructed and returning to the start of the job, it became evident that there were lots of worms all over the paths and that they appeared to be not at all well. This concoction was a worm killer as well as a weedkiller! My first reaction was to immediately fill a pail with water then proceed to pick up the worms and swill them off and return them back to the garden to recover from their trauma.

However, paths are not easy to keep free of weeds unless one has a solid foundation underneath of concrete or tarmac etc. The best alternative is a fairly powerful flame gun, but sodium chlorate or 'Amcide' will break down into sulphate of ammonia after a few months. Very small weeds can be killed with salt, but it becomes a continual process.

Semi-permanent paths can be constructed with polythene, bark chippings, carpet or a combination of the two.

BONFIRES

The question of burning up prunings/rubbish always arises at some time. Prunings can be dealt with very efficiently with a shredder, but models vary and unless it is possible to share a model the rule is, always buy a larger model that is capable of dealing with branches of at least 3 cms (1 inch) thick for preference. Some silent models are being developed at present and are worth looking out for; for a quiet life.

Most gardens will need a bonfire at some time; if not, burn some of the larger prunings or logs on the home fire, which is probably the best place.

The other method needs space and is easy in a large garden with a wood or spinney. It necessitates cutting prunings into a reasonable size and making a neat pile to rot down eventually in a natural way as in a typical woodland environment.

WOOD ASH

Wood ash is a useful product and contains generous amounts of potash and lime. It does vary according to the type of wood being burnt. Lime tree wood produces over 30% K_2O, with birch and oak only about 8% K_2O, beech 12%. Oak is high in calcium, 75% CaO; but beech and ash are 39% CaO. Wood ash should be used with caution and not too often as the soil can soon become sticky with a build-up of sodium.

3

The Organic Lawn

Wolterton Hall is situated in beautiful country with wooded grounds and a lake usually dominated by wild geese during winter, which fly continually, transferring themselves to and from the neighbouring Blickling Hall just half a mile from the lake.

The local church at Wickmere has a record of the Walpole family's vaults and tombs. The church has a round tower and a fifteenth-century screen.

Wolterton Hall was built in 1741 by Horatio Walpole. He employed Thomas Ripley as the architect, who also helped to design Houghton Hall for Sir Robert Walpole first Prime Minister of England. G.S. Repton was responsible for the design of the steps and veranda and steps at the back of the Hall. (Nephew of Humphrey Repton).

The opportunity arose in 1978 when a head gardener was required at Wolterton Hall. I attended an interview with Lord Walpole in the library. The family has a great ancestry and is proud of its most famous one, Lord Nelson; at least two rooms in the Hall were given to his memory.

Another upstairs room was devoted to the memory of St Henry Walpole and left untouched since he used it. He was one of the Forty Martyrs canonized in 1970 who had suffered death for conscience' sake during the sixteenth and seventeenth centuries.

As it turned out in the interview, the job consisted of quite a few extras, there being no living-in servants in the Hall to do the work of a butler or manservant. This would be the responsibility of myself and David, who knew all there was to know regarding procedure. We would be expected to open up the house before breakfast – this entailed folding back the wooden shutters to each window on the ground floor – emptying the kitchen bins, then proceeding down to the cellars, where there could be up to a dozen pairs of hunting boots to clean, as her ladyship hunted with the Quorn in Leicestershire once a week.

Lady Walpole was keen to keep flowers in all parts of the hall. Flowers were taken to the 'flower room'. Winter flowers come from the greenhouses, bronze chrysanthemums being a favourite. Carnations were used regularly with cyclamen and other pot plants, including *Chincherinchee ornithogalum* sent from South Africa, hyacinths and Paper White narcissus etc. Sweet peas were grown from a specialist breeder; planted in the autumn and grown by layering and pinching out tendrils, it was all very time consuming, but her ladyship insisted on using stems of sweet peas with no less than four blooms on each! Anything else was smartly discarded.

Zantedschia arum lilies are always useful for forcing ready for Easter, but need frost-free conditions before moving into heat. A large area of the garden was utilized by peonies, which were grown to sell in bud at the end of May–June.

The garden provided much greenery and flowers during the winter season: *Viburnum tinus, Hamamelis mollis*, hellebores, *Cornus mas, Arbutus unedo, Chimonanthus fragrans*.

All the logs of wood from the estate were stacked mature and ready for filling wicker baskets for each room; which we did. A very nice herd of Jerseys was kept on the farm and it was our duty to collect milk daily from the dairy. This we delivered to the Hall and also to the surrounding holiday flats nearby, whose occupants expected to have logs, milk and veg from the garden delivered, and their dustbins put out for collection. Two of these flats were in the Hall itself, on the first floor and connected to a lift; one was named after Nelson.

Apart from David and myself there was a team of land girls who worked on the estate on potato crops etc. but could help in the garden if the work got on top of us. The only other help was part-time, someone who lived in cottages nearby on the estate and was housed at a peppercorn rent to his lordship. Other jobs included washing the cars and Land Rover on Saturday mornings, winding the clock on the clock tower on alternate Sundays, providing fresh salads etc. for the Hall and, of course, the milk. One privilege for the head gardener was to clean the church silver on a Saturday afternoon, as necessary.

David had worked on the estate for 18 years and knew the ropes thoroughly. He was a jovial character who inevitably saw humour in most situations and a keen football supporter who never missed a match. He explained details of how to prepare vegetables for the house, which was most invaluable; such as small carrots only; or having a ready supply of onions for salads, substituting Welsh onions when spring ones were finished.

The walled-in garden consisted of at least four acres; some of it was used for horse paddocks but approximately two acres were cultivated. A walled glasshouse had seen better days but the peach house was excellent and contained two nectarines as well as peaches. There was also a small greenhouse used for tomatoes and chrysanthemums alternately; this was sunk approximately four feet deep, the most efficient way of utilizing heat, and well worth the extra expense.

The secret of starting the peaches off was to provide plenty of water in the spring; this they had been without all winter so they needed to be flooded, and his lordship was most emphatic in pointing this out one morning, rather to my surprise. But peaches need covering over winter to avoid 'peach leaf curl', otherwise they have to be sprayed with a copper fungicide.

Recently when considering peaches and pollination, it seems worthwhile to plant around the trees attractive flowering plants to attract bees. There are several perennials flowering in early spring which do the job very well on a nice sunny day. First is that ever flowering winter attraction *Helleborus foetidus*, which seeds generously and is easy to move about the garden.

In a south-facing aspect *Daphne odora* will also be in bloom, along with *Symphytum grandiflorum*; *Doronicum Spring Beauty*, or (leopard's bane,) which comes out in mid-March, should be in time. Another useful shrub flowering with peaches should be *Pieris japonica*, evergreen and easy to move around especially if grown in a pot.

The south side of the walled garden had two mature apricot

trees and alongside the paths were espalier apples, whilst a west wall had cordon pears, Morello cherries on the north wall, sweet cherries on the east. Between the garden and the Hall was a hard tennis court and alongside the wall *cytisus battenderii* grew to a generous ten feet or more. Past the beech hedge were rhododendrons which were brought down from Scotland but took 12 years to bloom again.

LAWNS

The lawn had grown a quantity of moss, but not wanting to waste the 'winter wash' usually used on fruit trees, (but not by organic gardeners) we used it to kill the moss. Other methods are to water on iron sulphate at 102 (28.35gms) sprayed – 2 gals per 16 sq yds or 2oz (56gms) used dry, which works very well, but the moss should be well raked/scarified first. Another method for moss eradication is to use 1 teaspoon of 'copper sulphate' dissolved in 45 litres (10 gal) water. This method sounds very cheap, but I have yet to try it. Fish blood and bonemeal is also a moss deterrent and a most useful feed. In the past coal ashes were used very effectively, wood ash also works in autumn but is not perhaps so reliable. The best killer of daisies is common salt and works 100%. Feeding is the secret of a good weed free lawn, but the lawn must be allowed to smother the weeds, which some may be sorry to hear means adjusting the mower to cut no less than 1 or 1½ or 2 inches (2.5, 3.75 or 5cm) is even better.

My own designed lawn spiker is most effective (see photograph); though a motorized version advertised regularly in the press as a general cultivator would be much easier to use, and better for a larger garden. Spiking the lawn provides aeration and if it does not help to reduce moss it certainly makes the grass grow.

The organic gardener needs to decide whether to tolerate a weedy lawn which could improve his compost or to rigidly keep it totally grass/clover or possibly to have a wild flower patch. Clover can be an asset to increase nitrogen and to resist the drought. Clover also has a strong tendency to smother unwanted weeds and is an asset to a cleaner lawn. Improving the lawn by rotavating, cleaning up and resowing it, is sometimes well worth the trouble. We then have the opportunity to start afresh and to sow some healthy seed most appropriate to the conditions, bearing in mind drought-resistant varieties, wearing tolerance and general disease resistance.

Choice of lawn grasses for specific purposes

Disease resistance

Brown Patch – tall fescue, the various rye grasses
Corticum/red thread (straw colour, pink) – fine fescues, Kentucky bluegrass, perennial ryegrass
Dollar Spot (brown or straw colour) – fine fescues, Kentucky bluegrass, perennial ryegrass
Fusarium Blight – Kentucky bluegrass – 10/15%, perennial ryegrass
Fusarium Patch (reddish brown colour) – fine fescue; Kentucky bluegrass (*poa pratensis* Smooth-Stalked Meadow Grass)

Drought tolerance

Tall fescue, red fescue, perennial ryegrass, *poa pratensis*, *cynosurus cristatus*, crested dogs tail, plus cover!

Shady areas

Poa annua, poa trivialis

Wearing tolerance

Meadow fescue; tall fescue; perennial ryegrass; Kentucky bluegrass poa Pratensis

Disease treatment

Brown patch – Prevalent in hot, humid weather. Garlic oil used at 0.02oz–0.03oz per gallon has inhibited the Mycelial growth in

Rhizoctonia Blight or Brown Patch, also known as 'Fusarium Patch'

Corticum/Red Thread – Use more nitrogen. Poultry manure recommended

Dollar Spot – Can be killed with fungicidal soap, but this should be spread over a period of 4–5 days as a drench would kill the grass

Snow Mould/Fusarium Patch/Grey Snow Mould – Can also be chemically controlled with iron sulphate. Using a solution of $\frac{1}{4}$oz (7g) ferrous iron sulphate in $\frac{1}{2}$ gallon (1.91g) water per square yard (0.84 sq m). Moisture should be used within $\frac{1}{2}$ hour as it soon reverts to its ineffective ferric form. Iron sulphate is a least toxic treatment and appears quite harmless to wildlife.

Fairy Ring – Use elder fungicide 3.5 l water 500g Elder leaves and simmer $\frac{1}{2}$ hour

Fusarian Blight – Use less $N°$

Toad Stools – Epsom salts

Weed indicators in the lawn

Clover (If not required) – Low $N°$, drought compaction. Weeds are encouraged by faulty management and the indications of their presence is shown

Thistles – The treatment for killing is restricted to rough land or meadows only. Eradication of thistle on meadow or rough land can be achieved by mowing as low as possible four times per year at monthly intervals for approximately 3 seasons

Dr W A Albrecht, Ph.D., microbiologist and soil scientist, University of Missouri, published papers (available from AG Access, P.O. Box 2008, Davis CA 95617. 515pp Raytown MO. Acres. USA) which are considered to be the most important book on soil fertility, highly regarded in the US. If his brilliant insights into the role of calcium, which plays such a big part in soil and plant health, had been heeded, it is said American agriculture would not be facing some of its current problems with soil degradation and groundwater pollution.

The first essential when dealing with weeds in the lawn is to test the soil. The latest scientific evidence from America suggests the importance of calcium; Dr Albrecht's study in the laboratory taking a particle of clay soil and removing all nutrient cations, then slowly adding them back found that there was a critical proportion of calcium relative to other mineral nutrients and that the proportion of cations that worked best was calcium 60%–75%, magnesium 10%–20%, nitrogen 10%, potassium 2–5%, sodium 0.5%–5%, others 5%. To reproduce this balance in the lawn, send a sample to a soil testing laboratory and request an analysis of the cation exchange capacity (or CEC). This indication is not concerned with the normal NPK test.

Most lawns are underfed and regarded as capable of looking after themselves, apart from mowing; but a good lawn needs as much care as the perennial border.

Nitrogen feed can be reduced by as much as 30% if clover is included in the grass. Again if a modern mower is used to mulch the grass clippings in, then less $N°$ is needed.

Autumn Lawn Dressing (amounts indicated in parts)

	Compost/leaf mould	Sand	Stacked turf/loam
heavy soils	1	4	2
loamy soils	1	2	4
light soils	2	1	4

Spring lawn feed

An excellent feed at almost anytime would be calcified seaweed, which is fortified with magnesium. But a most practical feed for spring/summer is a liquid seaweed extract; this is a foliar feed, so it is quick-acting. Urine is also a quick-acting feed; it has 10–15% nitrogen plus potassium; it is mixed at 10–1 with water as a feed or used neat to kill weeds. Though it is a great mistake to overestimate nitrogen any more than for a spring flush, it needs to be in proportion to phosphate and potash. To complement the former, a liquid feed of comfrey would also be a supplement or an alternative – thus providing potash plus.

17

Wild flower lawn

This type of planting involves two types of flower. First the very wild, mostly poppies, yarrow, cowslips and plants not common to a cultivated garden which grow very well in a meadow. They need poor soil and should be planted with meadow grasses free from ryegrass, such as creeping bent and fescue grasses, for the best effect.

Seed houses specializing in natural wild flower seed production offer several seed mixes combining wild flower/grass meadow mixes (see appendix) and are only too pleased to give advice on suitable mixtures for dry or wet conditions, etc.

The second type of planting concerns plants from the normal perennial border but which are able to look after themselves, in a less formal way of planting; this is a new and most interesting development which has arisen from new ways of planting in Europe. Generally described as 'the new perennial garden', this type of planting involves most methods but makes the best use of a plant's ecological conditions. For instance on looking around in hedgerows and road banks it is not hard to find strong perennials growing in association with grass and other 'plants in the wrong place'!

My recent experience with goats rue, *Galega officinalis*, tells me that it is quite a formidable plant, quite capable of holding its own against any of the common grasses. It is quite easy to find border geraniums growing happily along the roadside, especially *Geranium Macrorrhizum* etc. Another quite formidable plant, *Lysimachia vulgaris* – yellow loose-strife – can be seen quite frequently along roadside verges.

Although the average border plant is not often seen growing elsewhere, at least in this country, many of them are prolific. Some are described as thugs or pigs, so they would suit rougher conditions quite happily. However, they are not all suited to the same environment. So some thought as to their preference needs to be given, such as wet or dry soil, shade or sun.

The system originating in Europe and now receiving great interest in this country emphasizes natural planting, reminding us of such great gardeners as William Robinson who longed to get away from the 'formalities' of the gardening world. There are many different aspects in which the new planting regime works, so what are the considerations for an organic gardener?

Firstly the system is organic, a natural approach; it encourages wildlife birds and predators. (Most plantings consist of at least 50% or more from the Compositae/Umbelliferae families better known as the carrot and daisy families.) They can be selected according to individual taste; giant grasses and ferns can be very beautiful in their place. Especially on a frosty morning in mid-winter or with dew on them, grasses can look most striking. Grasses also perform well as weed suppressers. The whole approach is highly practical especially when planting. All areas can be catered for, from a garden lawn to rough factory sites or wooded areas meadows etc. using a minimum of labour and effort. In planting up a lawn, holes may be dug, removing turf and adding compost with adequate spacing; then continue cutting the grass as previously until the plants take hold, or on rough areas use a strim-mer. For the first year or so a close watch should be kept on the plants with this method.

Other rougher areas smothered with rubbish, e.g. brambles or twitch, may need slashing back and then rotavating over, for a reasonable tilth. Rough grass areas and meadows can be carpeted over with newspaper plus straw or leaf mould; black polythene can be used very effectively over a period of at least four months, to allow the turf to rot and allow planting to take place.

Plug plants have also been used recently with wild flowers etc, but the ground needs to be kept very clean for a successful planting.

Progress in the new perennial garden can be quite rapid and well worthwhile providing a complete transformation.

Maintenance will be necessary to remove and compost spent flowers and stalks. This is best done in the new year rather than autumn, to provide wildlife with seeds, and allow insects to over-winter on stalks etc. Hoeing around plants or even digging until the ground is covered may be necessary in the early years. Plants such as *Hypericum calycinum* are sure weed smotherers, and there are quite a selection of good ground cover plants available for using in between plantings to ease the weed situation.

This new concept of gardening could be the beginning of a healing atmosphere in the garden. Most of us at some time or other are subject to stress, too much hustle and bustle, and in need of quiet, a place of meditation, a sanctuary for rest, a garden seat where we are able to just look and listen. All these desirable qualities of life become open to us by readjusting a garden layout to suit our needs.

The late Geoff Hamilton discovered in some of his last TV appearances the 'Gardens of Paradise'; they were a source of great beauty, peace and quiet and he very often showed the example at the end of a series, relaxing in an arbour and for once forgetting about the necessities of a garden but rather just witnessing it.

As the Very Rev. Michael Stancliffe, Dean of Winchester, wrote in his Saturday *Telegraph* column called 'Meditation':

Garden Paths to God

To be led up the garden path is to be led astray. We owe this proverbial phrase to the Serpent. But if it is God and not

Satan who leads, the path will bring us to nothing but good. And most of us will find such a path congenial, for we are garden-lovers at heart; no less than 85 per cent of Britain's householders have a garden. It is almost instinctive to tend the plots of earth around our homes and cherish the plants we choose to grow in them. No trivial part of inner city misery is being deprived of the chance to satisfy that instinct.

Man's love of gardens is reflected in the Bible which begins with a garden and ends with a garden-city. Other familiar biblical gardens are the Garden of Gethsemane and that in which Jesus was buried and where Mary Magdalene met him after his resurrection. There was Naboth's vineyard which Ahab coveted for his own herb garden (1 Kings 21.2); the garden which God would make of the desert (Isaiah 35); the great garden described in Ecclesiastes (2. 4–5); the garden repeatedly referred to in the Song of Solomon. At least one of the parables of Jesus concerns a garden problem (Luke 13. 6–9), and others make a direct appeal to gardeners as well as farmers. And throughout both Testaments there are many references to garden work – digging, dunging, sowing, planting, weeding, staking, pruning, and so on.

Many religious writers have found gardens fertile ground for symbols with which to illustrate their teaching. Just how luxuriant a garden the Christian imagination can become may be gauged from the fact that St Bernard wrote no less than 80 sermons on the first two chapters of the Song of Solomon and its garden! There is certainly a theme here which God can use to feed our thinking and praying for the next three months. Ruminate on the words of Paul for a start: 'You are God's garden' (1 Corinthians 3.9 in the New English Bible).

4

Shotesham Sale

The lawn at Wolterton is bounded on one side by a ha-ha which gives a pleasant view across to the lake usually inhabited by thousands of geese, but it has been known to be jumped by a most energetic racehorse who promptly made her mark on the front lawn if not anywhere else, much to the annoyance of us gardeners.

The soil at Wolterton is a very fertile loam. Described as a neutral brick earth, it grows rhododendrons and azaleas quite successfully, they need dead-heading as they finish blooming to form good strong blooms for the following year. Rhododendrons can also be quite prolific and rapidly outgrow a large area, often to the detriment of the less prolific azalea, and drastic pruning is the only remedy. Which reminds me of the royal gardens at Windsor Great Park, which have such magnificent displays of rhododendrons. Some years ago when viewing them, I happened upon a nice little seedling growing on a pathway beside an exotic *rhododendron, Ilam Cream*, a gorgeous yellow shrub, which I promptly removed into my pocket in the hopes of a repeat; only to find that in a year's time it turned out to be *Rhododendron ponticum*!

A small corner in one of the walled gardens at Wolterton had been planted with apples which had hardly been pruned since planting. It was plain to see that 'apple sucker' had been destroying fruit buds, treated at that time with a tar distillate, which of course kills other predators as well as the apple suckers. Nicotine or quassia would be less harmful but *Athocoris nemorum* is the main predator for this, as well as aphids, scale insects, midges, capsids and small caterpillars. They can be encouraged with

Compositae and Umbelliferae plants and a general increase in mulching with composts/farmyard manure to build up the general ecology around the fruit trees. One tree in particular had a ring of bark practically eaten away by some animal which would eventually be fatal, but there is a method of grafting a young cutting and bridging it over the barkless circle, thus retaining the sap from below to above the wound until the bark grows over it again; this was done successfully.

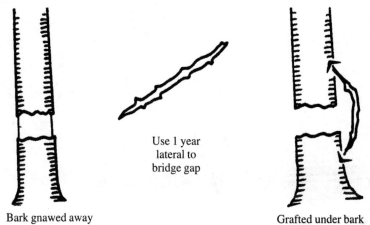

Bark gnawed away

Use 1 year
lateral to
bridge gap

Grafted under bark

The woolly aphis is perhaps the worst bug of fruit trees, it not only ruins a crop but also causes canker. Using methylated spirit is not very effective, so this year I have now turned to a good 'waste oil'; painted on with a brush it is most effective. This, incidentally, is also a good cure against mealy bugs and scale insects on peaches or oleanders.

My recent experience concerning fruit trees and the most common pests such as codlin moths, points to having such plants as rosemary, wormwood (*Artemesia absinthium*); Santolina, southernwood (*Artemisia abrotanum*) and mint in close proximity to the trees. Their scent is very strong and particularly unpleasant to moths. Codlin moth traps are also a useful aid, using one trap per five trees.

Whilst I was at Wolterton, in September 1979, the contents from Shotesham Hall, previously owned by Major Fellows,

23

whose ancestor William Fellows in 1771 founded the first cottage hospital in England, were sold by Christie's the auctioneers. It was quite an important event, certainly as far as the contents of the library were concerned. My mother and I attended the sale. We wandered through a most roomy library with such books set out on the tables before us as Jethro Tull's *The Home Hoeing Husbandry*, several books by the agriculturalist and much travelled Arthur Young, Sir Joseph Paxton's *Magazine of Botany* (sold for £2,800) and John Gerard's *Herball* (sold for £2,850). My mother spotted a gardening book she thought she might like – it was Philip Miller's figures of plants described in the *Gardener's Dictionary* in two volumes, 1755–60, which eventually sold for £3,500, I believe to the Lindley Library. Philip Miller's *Gardener's Dictionary*, in a smaller edition, had previously sold for £400. We had also seen David Hume's *Treatise of Human Nature*, 1740 (of which the British Library also possessed a copy) sell for £4,700. Quite enough for one day but not forgotten.

Back in the garden, the tomatoes in a sunken greenhouse had a lot of white fly and I well remember approaching his lordship on the question of biological control, but when it was explained that we should be using some little *Encarsia formosa*, parasitic wasps, flying on the tomatoes, his lordship was horrified and would not hear of it. So he installed an electric insecticidal humidifier, which we thought most unsuitable. However, nowadays we use French marigolds if it is not possible to use *Encarsia formosa*, which need at least 45°F. Wireworms and slugs are repelled by the smell of the common marigold, whose flower heads also make an 'antiseptic' wash when picked and brewed. Marigolds also are good with roses and narcissus bulbs as they repel the nematodes especially associated with rose sickness.

The walled-in garden at Wolterton Hall is now organic and run by Barker Organics, which has a box scheme in the area. David Barker intends to rejuvenate the garden and gradually bring it back to its former glory. But the peach house, although rather dilapidated, still produces a massive crop of peaches from the old plants. He is using sheep as well as a few chickens to keep up fertility, all enhancing its lovely situation.

COMPANION PLANTS

Which brings me to the subject of plant alleopathy and the use of another marigold as a weed deterrent, namely *Tagetes minuta*, which has such a powerful effect on other plants, especially ground elder (*Aegopodium podagraria*) which it kills quite effectively.

Perhaps the other greatest problem with companion planting is the onion (*Allium*), which seems to be alien to most plants. My latest discovery is mustard, a sure victim of incompatibility with onions. Other interesting plants of this category are especially the walnut (*Juglans nigra*), which is also a killer, especially of tomatoes, blackberry, alfalfa, asparagus, dock, potato, cereals, pine and apple trees and chrysanthemum, but which does tolerate such plants as plums, Kentucky bluegrass, pear trees, ferns, asters, wild grape, clover, buckwheat and peach.

It is most useful to be able to select plants for their companionships and where they will grow most compatibly one with another to demonstrate good neighbourliness.

At a first glance at a companion planting chart, one soon discovers that some plants are more compatible than others. Take for instance the potato, which hates to be near apple trees or apricots, dislikes courgettes and cucumbers, pumpkins and raspberries, squash and sunflowers and, yes, even tomatoes. But it grows very well with pulse crops, having no regard either way for runner beans. Potatoes can be conveniently grown next to celery and celeriac, or in between rows without upsetting the rotation. They are most favourably grown with brassicas and also like the companionship of herbs such as summer savory, tarragon, parsley, mint, horseradish or lavender, not forgetting sweetcorn and strawberries. So they do have their preferences, whereas simple parsnip has only one unfavourable associate – sweet pepper – but favours garlic. There are other plants such as catmint, cherry, currant, gooseberry, marigold and a few more which have virtually no enemies but quite a few beneficial partners; these are well worth remembering.

Planting a few chives in the strawberry bed has a favourable effect in reducing botrytis, and any spare patches can easily be filled with some lettuce, which grows well with strawberries.

Spinach, strawberry, tomato, sunflower and runner bean do not like the brassica family. Onions do not go with the pulse family but will go with carrots, like leeks, which are also of the onion family. They are good for warding off the carrot fly.

5

Plants versus Pests

Using plants to their fullest extent in our quest to maintain an even balance between the build-up of pests and predators and also to minimise pests, there are two important groups – attractant plants and detractant plants. The former consist of Asteraceae (Compositae) daisy types and Apiaceae (Umbelliferae), which are mostly parsley/carrot types. The latter are often the smellier plants, which discourage bugs like moths or aphis. They are fewer and far between, but consist of plants like *Artemisia absinthium* (wormwood) to repel moths, flea beetles, cabbage butterfly and flies. *Artemisia abrotanum* (southernwood) repels aphis, also moths. Garlic is often effective as a spray but is good planted amongst roses as a repellent against aphis, and as an encouragement to stronger scent.

If broad beans are planted in spring then they should be accompanied by summer savory as a precaution against black fly. Rosemary, hyssop and thyme also discourage cabbage butterflies, but we need to experiment with planting to camouflage the scent of brassicas and avoid monoculture planting.

A system which is most congenial for small beds is a vegetable potager, where good use can be made of herbs and vegetables together.

Whatever system is used it is better to have vegetables in small groups, thus camouflaging scents and deceiving cabbage butter-flies etc. Edging a plot with euonymus or box hedge looks neat and tidy but box does encourage slugs etc underneath. So having looked into the more healthy plants, it seems appropriate to use dwarf lavender, such as *Lavandula angustifolia* 40cm H × 23cm W or 16 × 9 inches, Little Lottie – there are many varieties to choose from and they are virtually pest free. Good use can also be made of thyme, rosemary and hyssop; what a practical edging they make! *Hyssopus officionalis* has very nice white or blue flowers and is mentioned quite freely in the Bible: 'Purge me with hyssop and I shall be clean' (though this plant is known as *Hyssopus aristatus* and is a more compact plant, but used a great deal for medicinal requirements in biblical times).

NATURAL RESISTANCE

During the last 30 or 40 years a lot has developed towards plant resistance to disease. Thompson and Morgan's marketing of the first carrot to resist the carrot fly was a major breakthrough for most of us. Although only one of the smaller variety of carrots, Fly Away is a great asset and saves a lot of trouble in guarding against the fly.

Merely glancing through seed catalogues, it is easy to pinpoint various varieties with disease resistance unheard of a few years ago: tomatoes with a Soil Association symbol resistant to such problems as tobacco mosaic virus, cladosporium A to E, verticillium, fusarium race 1 & 2, greenback etc. We now have 140 varieties of tomato to choose from in just one catalogue, varying from beefsteaks to Tiny Tim and red cherries, Green Zebra, Persimmon Orange, Yellow Perfection, pear-shaped Roma and Sausage. Or there are Black Russian and Green Grape.

Parsnips more resistant to canker, though one variety grown for many years, Tender & True, now seems to have succumbed to canker, give way to Avonresister, White Gem or Gladiator, which have a better resistance.

But potatoes have always been a challenge. Which one to grow? And for what purpose? If we choose a high-yielding variety then it will almost certainly lack flavour; if it is resistant to blight then it may be a coarse variety or give way to spraig. If we choose the best flavour it will sure to be a poor yielder or an unhealthy potato. Is there such a thing as a perfect potato? Perhaps for flavour but certainly not from a grower's point of view. Micro propagation has been a great boost to 'clean up' some of the older varieties from the many viruses that potatoes so easily get, especially if not grown from healthy Scotch seed.

Some recent introductions show great promise especially against blight which is probably the most troublesome disease of potatoes.

The Department of Agriculture & Fisheries in Scotland holds 700 varieties of potato for potential breeding and experiment. It is also possible to choose from over 100 different varieties each year from 'potato days' held in various parts of the country. The modern potato has improved a great deal in yield potential, rising dramatically from an average in 1945 of 7.2 tonnes per acre to 18.4 tonnes per acre in 1992. Salad potatoes have now become popular especially among the discerning or connoisseur eater but Fir Apple types are much smaller in size and therefore less profitable, also less healthy.

The future of the potato for organic growing looks bright with the emphasis on the newer varieties which can only improve on many older varieties, some of which remained in the mind especially during the war years. In the forties it was something of a permanent ritual in my schoolboy years enquiring from my farming relations as to what variety they were growing; the answer was usually 'Oh Majestic, of course!' This was a variety that lasted as Britain's No. 1 from 1945 to 1960 when it gained 43% of the market. Today's best red potatoes for popularity are Desiree and Romano, both with blight resistance.

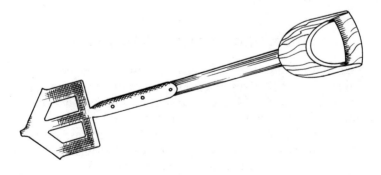

In 1998 the BBC's *Gardening World* tested eight new varieties against slug damage.

Kestrel	came out top with no damage from slugs, good flavour, resistant to blackfly, mosaic virus, golden eelworm, and drought and is a 2nd early.
Charlotte	had only 5.6 damage from slugs. 2nd early.
Valor	has overall resistance to blight and double eelworm. Main crop.
Stirling	had good resistance to blight. Main crop.
Charlotte	well recommended for flavour; healthy, waxy type.
Roseval	salads; healthy, excellent flavour, red.

Interesting new varieties

Harmony	2nd early. Very high yield, waxy; eelworm and scab resistant.
Karlena	1st early. Frying, baking or roasting. Very disease resistant.
Marfona	2nd early. Baker, tubers large, av blight resistance.
Mondial	Main crop, good disease resistance. Good on poor soil.
Morene	Early main crop, large tubers, baking or chipping. Very good disease resistantance.
Picasso	Early main crop, high yielding, good disease resistance.
Winston	1st early, high yielding, baker. Very good disease resistance.

NEW, OLD AND RARE VARIETIES

Thanks to micropropagation (plants grown in sterile conditions in test tubes, free from virus disease) some of the forgotten varieties of potato are now available as seedlings or young plants. They are invaluable for new plant breeding material; some are a mere novelty such as one called 'Congo' 1900. A late main crop closely related to the wild species, with small knobbly tubers and shiny black-violet skin. It turns violet with maturity.

One variety called 'Skerry Blue' 1846 a main crop, has rich violet blue skin with cream coloured flesh. Described with a superb flavour and good blight resistance!

Forty fold is a late main crop. 1836 was a popular Victorian speciality. The tubers are irregular a vivid purple splashed white, of excellent eating quality with good blight resistance.

At least two seedsmen are offering these delights of the past, including the organic catalogue – Henry Doubleday Research Association. Many of these old varieties could well make a re-appearance in a short time by popular demand.

For lifting potatoes the best tool yet devised is the Irish potato fork, especially if tubers are inclined to 'spike' – very difficult to avoid using the average fork. (See illustration.)

This year my latest is Remarka, which is said to be an advance in two or three ways. Time will tell as to its suitability for my light, poor soil.

COMFREY

But to grow both tomatoes and potatoes well we do need comfrey, the plant one could not miss when joining the Henry Doubleday Association in 1975 and to which it was totally dedicated. Laurence Hills had sorted a hybrid plant from its many variations which he named as Bocking 14, a most prolific plant reaching 4 to 5 feet high with very high potassium level, nitrogen and phosphate VB12, silica and the healing ingredient allantoin.

This year for the first time comfrey was introduced into a large garden which I look after. I had previously used the liquid manure Tomorite, so it was possible to make a comparison having fed this year totally on comfrey liquid. I found very little difference except perhaps this year there was a slight increase in the amount of tomatoes per truss. Comfrey is so prolific as to afford up to five or six cuttings per year of its fleshy bulky leaves either used in its leaf form 'dug in' or put into a container for ten days to provide a liquid foliar feed. Either way it provides the nourishment needed for any potash-hungry plants, including cucurbits etc.

Comfrey makes an excellent healthy stock food replacing protein and has great potential against E coli infections so prevalent on farms today. So much so as to be highly recommended in the prevention of E coli infection, both in humans and in stock!

All the varieties of comfrey make a good addition to the compost heap as activators, quickly rotting down and speeding fermentation. Broad beans demand a high level of potash in order to resist chocolate spot, and therefore comfrey makes an excellent accompaniment especially if sowing them in late autumn, so using the last of the comfrey leaves before they disappear for winter.

VEGETABLE RESISTANCE

Several varieties of peas are now mildew resistant, including an old one, Greenshaft, which is also resistant to fusarium wilt. Other interesting newer varieties include Cavalier main crop. Onward main crop is an old variety, and Kelvedon Wonder is also an old variety and mildew resistant. The new Ambassador is resistant to mildew, enation virus and fusarium wilt.

Also in the vegetable garden we now have a good selection of more resistant varieties: French beans resistant to mosaic virus, beetroot resistant to bolting, and Brussels sprouts resistant to powdery mildew (something which has not troubled me).

One variety which has proved most useful which came from the HDRA seed library is a cos lettuce Brown Golding. It overwinters and will be the first to taste in the new year with a better flavour than most of the modern ones.

6

Roses

Turning to the flower garden and consideration of more healthy plants, we need to remember that good husbandry is also most important for the plant to give of its best. This applies more to roses than perhaps other plants. They are the most difficult plants to grow, especially hybrid teas, modern floribundas and miniatures, in fact the more continuous flowering roses.

A rose catalogue from Peter Beales, London Road, Attleborough, who hold the National Collection of Rosa Species, is an excellent start on selecting roses, giving full details on the right roses for flowering; tub or pot; tolerance of poor soils; those for hedges, hips, north walls, shade, autumn foliage. Choosing roses suitable for poor soils is half the battle to growing a successful rose on sandy light soils.

In consideration of species roses we are led to some of the most interesting of old roses, those to which all modern roses trace their ancestry.

Rosa alba the 'white rose of York' (6ft × 4ft – 1.8m × 1.2m) has reddish-orange fruit. Pre-sixteenth century, it is probably the oldest *alba*. *Albas* are some of the healthiest roses, all are reliable. This family includes the *Rosa anemoneflora* 1844 species, an almost thornless, medium-growing climber, with white double flowers (12ft × 8ft – 4m × 2.9m). *Albas* are early flowering and mostly lightly scented.

Among the species one stands out with great dignity, usually making itself known in some of the larger stately homes. This is *Rosa moyesii* (1928) and its hybrid *Rosa highdownensis* (8ft × 6ft

– 2.4m × 1.8m) with small healthy leaves, flowers of light crimson producing abundant flagon-shaped hips. Rugosas rank amongst the most healthy roses, both single and double, scented. Many are just 3 – 4ft × under 6ft (0.9m – 1.2m × 1.8m) with occasional hips.

Rosa moschata (8ft × 6ft – 2.4m × 1.8m) white, flowering from mid-July, fragrant, with grey foliage, was used by the Rev. J.H. Pemberton in the breeding of his hybrid musks. Useful for short border or hedging and notably free from disease, they need pruning only if plants become 'leggy'. *R. Rambling Rector* is also an offspring of the same family, or the white Shakespeare's Musk (25ft × 15ft – 7.5m × 4.5m).

As organic gardeners we need trouble-free roses; when selecting it is easy to be enticed into buying for colour or shape, many of us are gullible and buy poor quality roses. The flower show is only interested in its exhibits and no questions are asked as to the rest of the plant. Black spot can be serious and spoil the look of an otherwise good rose; mildew can be even worse and weather considerations are always important, but in fine summer weather roses are not affected by adverse wet and cold.

A rose such as *R. Iceberg* has weathered extremely well, but is reputed to suffer from mildew. In my experience it needs plenty of free flowing air around it and should not be planted in a too sheltered spot.

Recently we decided to buy one or two thornless roses for a fence and I am glad to say all are growing healthy and well – one is *R. Lykkefund*, a rambler with semi double creamy flowers in clusters (15ft × 12ft – 4.5m × 3.6m). The other is *R. Ghislaine de Feligonde*, with clusters of orange double, which can be used as a bush with support. (8ft × 8ft – 2.4m × 2.4m). The other thornless rose we inherited is named *R. Zephirine Drouhin*; it is over a hundred years old (1868 introduction). It is a bourbon rose and therefore should be pruned as such, which entails merely taking a length of briar and shortening its laterals to approx 4 inches all the way up. Mine has never needed spraying!

Something out of the ordinary is *R. Veilchenblau*, which verges on blue or mauve, is healthy and propagates quite easily (12ft – 3.5m-high).

Roses have generally improved in health in recent years. More attention has been given to disease-free roses, and during the 1980s new ground cover roses were introduced. These were repeat-flowering varieties under 2ft (0.6m) high but with a greater spread. They are an excellent choice for trouble-free roses, those named after counties – R. Suffolk, R. Surrey, R. Essex, R. Kent – are very commendable, as well as R. Red Bells, R. White & R. Pink Bells, excellent little roses which have the same parentage.

One of the first roses of the year to bloom is the shrub rose R. Canary Bird; in May it produces dainty yellow blooms lasting about one month (10ft – 3m high).

One of the most beautiful shrub roses one could wish to see would be R. Madame Hardy, a damask. This one is very healthy, a double white, with fragrance to match (5–6ft – 1.5m–1.8m high). It could be a martyr to rain or strong winds. But highly recommended.

To complement a recently planted hedge I planted R. Scharlaglut (Scarlet Fire). With strong stems reaching 9ft (2.7m) in height, it has a number of uses, being dense and thorny, and tolerant of shade. It can climb a tree, has hips for bird food and is most healthy. Another most commendable rose of the same colour is R. La Sevillana, with bright red semi double blooms which do not fade. It is a free-flowering modern shrub with good disease resistance, and weather tolerant. Another particular favourite is R. Elmshorn, a vivid pink, 5 × 4ft, modern shrub, with large clusters of small vivid pink flowers. The older roses seem to be more healthy than most of the modern ones. Black spot is more prevalent in wet seasons and as it is a virus which can spread from one season to another, one rose can infect another. But rose powdery mildew is more prevalent in dry, sheltered situations, especially by a wall. There are many excellent hybrid teas and floribundas coming on to the market. Choosing for health is difficult, but certain well-tried varieties are certainly more resistant than the average to both diseases mentioned.

DISEASE RESISTANT ROSES INTRODUCED
10 OR MORE YEARS AGO

Hybrid Tea

SILVER JUBILEE	(90cm)	Coppery pink, shaded peach; fragrant; free-flowering; keeps colour
SAVOY HOTEL	(90cm)	Pink; slightly fragrant; bedding, cutting or forcing under glass
ROYAL WILLIAM	(100cm)	Deep crimson; fragrant; good for flower arranging
REMEMBER ME	(90cm)	Coppery orange, blended yellow; slightly fragrant; offspring of Silver Jubilee/Alexander
GRANDPA DICKSON	(75cm)	Lemon yellow, edged pink; slightly fragrant; good rain resistance
ALECS RED	(90cm)	Cherry red; very fragrant; good rain resistance; many awards
BLESSINGS	(92cm)	Coral pink; slightly fragrant; ideal bedder; glossy foliage
CONGRATULATIONS	(130cm)	Rose pink; slightly fragrant; growth lanky, not a bedder
DEEP SECRET	(90cm)	Deep crimson; very fragrant
PEADOUCE (Elina)	(100cm)	Ivory, pale yellow base; fragrant; very highly praised; good all weathers
GOLDEN JUBILEE	(90cm)	Yellow; slightly fragrant; did not become a star; reliable
GOLD STAR	(90cm)	Deep yellow; slightly fragrant; colour does not fade, flowers high up
INDIAN SUMMER	(58cm)	Creamy orange; very fragrant; won award for fragrance, good rain resister, displays hips
INGRID BERGMAN	(80cm)	Deep red; fragrant; flowers last in water; many awards
JUST JOEY	(75cm)	Coppery orange; fragrant; world's favourite 1994, rain resistant
L'OREAL TROPHY	(120cm)	Orange; slightly fragrant; attractive foliage; a Sport of Alexander
ALEXANDER	(150cm)	Vermilion red; slightly fragrant; rain resistant; pointed centre flowers

LOVELY LADY	(75cm)	Rose pink; fragrant; bedding rose; large flowers
LOVING MEMORY	(100cm)	Red; slightly fragrant; said to be the ideal rose for every garden
LOVERS MEETING	(90cm)	Tangerine orange; slightly fragrant; foliage on strong stems
PINK FAVORITE	(75cm)	Deep pink; slightly fragrant; high on the list of disease free roses
POLAR STAR	(100cm)	White; slightly fragrant; Rose of Year 1985; considered best white rose
POT OF GOLD	(75cm)	Old gold; fragrant; great weather resistance; free flowering
ROSE GAUJARD	(100cm)	Rose red, silver reverse; slightly fragrant; lovely colour, plus all the best points
SAVOY HOTEL	(90cm)	Pink; slightly fragrant; good parents, a favourite
THE McCARTNEY ROSE	(100cm)	Deep pink; very fragrant; a top rose
TROIKA	(90cm)	Orange bronze, shaded red; fragrant; an unusual lovely copper colour
VELVET FRAGRANCE	(100cm)	Deep red; bred for fragrance, long flowering season
VIDAL SASSOON	(75cm)	Tan, shaded lavender; very fragrant; flower arranger's rose; unique colour

Patio Roses

ANNA FORD	(45cm)	Deep orange, yellow eye; slightly fragrant; floribunda miniature hybrid
SWEET DREAM	(40cm)	Apricot; fragrant Rose of Year 1988; rain resistant

Floribunda

AMBER QUEEN	(60cm)	Yellow; fragrant; many awards, 40 petals, glossy foliage
ANNE HARKNESS	(120cm)	Apricot yellow; slightly fragrant; good for late flowering, August onward
ANISLEY DICKSON	(90cm)	Salmon pink; slightly fragrant; numerous flowers; top honours in 1984

BEAUTIFUL BRITAIN	(75cm)	Tomato red; slightly fragrant; unusual colour, appealing
CITY OF LONDON	(90cm)	Blush pink; very fragrant; outstanding perfume, tight flowers, 18 petals
HARVEST FAYRE	(75cm)	Apricot orange; slightly fragrant; later flowering, strong growth
KORRESIA	(75cm)	Bright yellow; fragrant; blooms over a long period; star of roses
INVINCIBLE	(60cm)	Bright red; fragrant; good weather resistance
MOUNTBATTEN	(130cm)	Mimosa yellow; fragrant; a big rose, very healthy, hedger etc.
MANTANGI	(90cm)	Vermilion reverse silver; slightly fragrant; well-shaped buds; resistant to rain
MELODY MAKER	(70cm)	Vermilion; fragrant; V-shapely buds, 30 petals; Rose of the Year 1991
SOUTHAMPTON	(95cm)	Apricot orange; slightly fragrant; a good robust rose; lovely colour
REMEMBRANCE	(70cm)	Red; slightly fragrant; blooms continually; compact
TRUMPETER	(55cm)	Bright vermilion; slightly fragrant; front row bedder; heads bow in rain
TOPROSE (DANIA)	(82cm)	Bright yellow; slightly fragrant; Scottish bred, remarkably disease resistant
CHANELLE	(75cm)	Cream, flushed buff and pink; fragrant; above average resistance to mildew
ANNA LIVIA	(75cm)	Pink; slightly fragrant; leathery leaves; good all round bedder

Modern Shrubs

FRED LOADS	(2m)	Orange Vermilion; single; fragrant; repeat flowering, unfading blooms
FRITZ NOBIS	(2m)	Pink, double; slightly fragrant; mid-summer flowering; orange hips
GRAHAM THOMAS	(1.2m)	Deep yellow; double fragrant; repeat flowering until autumn; unusual flowers

38

CERISE BOUQUET	(3.5× 3.5m)	Double bright cerise flowers are produced in profusion on long, arching branches amid dense greyish-green foliage.
HERITAGE	(1.2m)	Pale pink; double; very fragrant; good reputation; flowers until autumn
LA SEVILLANA	(1.2m)	Scarlet; semi double; slightly fragrant; wide spreading, recommended
PEARL DRIFT	(1m×1m)	Whitish pink; semi double; no fragrance; glossy foliage
ROSERAIE DE L'HAY	(2.2m× 1.8m)	double wine red; fragrant Rugosa; good hedger; poor soil; prolific; repeat flowering
ELMSHORN	(2m×1m)	Vivid pink; non fragrant; tolerant of poor soil; late repeat flowering
ERFURT	(1m×1m)	Pink and white; slight fragrance; long flowering period
ROUNDELAY	(1m×1m)	Double; cardinal red; fragrant; upright, free flowering; tolerant of poor soil
CELESTIAL	(2m×1m)	Soft pink; fragrant; alba; highly recommended
WINCHESTER CATHEDRAL	(1m×1m)	White; very fragrant; continuous flowering

Species Roses

ROSA VIRGINIANA	(1.7m×1m)	Fragrant rich clear pink; single small flowers; plump red hips; excellent autumn leaf colour; good on sandy soil
ROSA RUBRIFOLIA	(2m×1.7m)	Single pink; plum grey foliage; good hips; fine for hedge
ROSA FARGESII	(2.2m× 1.7m)	Clear pink; large fruit; orange red, flagon-shaped
ROSA ALBA PLENA	(4.5m× 2.4m)	Double white; thornless; vigorous, climber
ROSA BANKSIAE LUTEA	(6m×3m)	Double yellow; climber; sunny; sheltered wall;. early flowering, over by June
ROSA BANKSIAE LUTESCENS	(6m×3m)	Single yellow; fragrant; climber, leaves and shoots copper-tinted

Climbers/Ramblers

BANTRY BAY	(3m)	Semi double pink; slight fragrance; repeat flowers; not rampant, restrained
DORTMUND	(3m)	Single red, white eye; fragrant; repeat flowering; glossy foliage, big flowers
DUBLIN BAY	(3m)	Double deep red; slight fragrance; beautifully formed flowers
GALWAY BAY	(3m)	Double pink; slight fragrance; large well formed flowers in profusion
GOLDEN SHOWERS	(3m)	Double yellow; fragrant; good resistance to rain
KIFTSGATE	(7m)	Single, creamy white; fragrant; big in every way, very good show
MADAME GREGOIRE (Spanish Beauty) STAECHELIN	(6m)	Double pink, shaded crimson; very fragrant; short season; smothered with blooms plus hips
MEG	(2.2m×1m)	Single, russet red, buff-yellow, apricot; fragrant; outstandingly beautiful
NEW DAWN	(3m)	Shell pink; fragrant; rambler of many uses
NIGHT LIGHT	(3m)	Double deep yellow; slight fragrance; likes the sun, not shade
PAUL'S HIMALAYAN MUSK	(7m+)	Double blush pink; slight fragrance; happy in partial shade
RAMBLING RECTOR	(7m+)	Semi double creamy white; fragrant; good on trees, north walls; hips
SEAGULL	(7m)	Single white; fragrant; rambler; grey-green foliage
WEDDING DAY	(7m)	Single creamy white; fragrant; flowers July & August; very big
ZEPHIRINE DROUHIN	(3m)	Semi double, cerise pink; very fragrant
WHITE COCKADE	(2m)	Double white; fragrant; not very big, but beautifully formed flowers
WICKWAR	(5m)	Single creamy white; dense growth; impressive in flower, plus orange hips

Modern Shrub

CHINATOWN	(1.5m)	Double yellow, flushed pink; fragrant; rain resistant, tolerates exposure
FOUNTAIN	(1.5m×1m)	Double crimson; fragrant; free flowering; tolerant of poor soil
CERISE BOUQUET	(4m×4m)	Clusters of pinkish-crimson; summer flowering; greyish foliage

Rosa Gallica

JAMES MASON	(1.1m×1m)	Rich bright crimson; fragrant; profuse flowering from mid-June
ROSA MUNDI	(1m×1m)	Semi double splashes of pink on white on a crimson background; 12th century
ROSA GALLICA OFFICINALIS	(1m×1m)	Semi double; light crimson; fragrant; June flowering, of great antiquity

ROSE CARE

A certain amount of good gardening is needed to maintain a healthy rose garden. Roses are notoriously heavy feeders whatever soil they grow on. Probably the best roses are grown in Essex on the heavy clay land, but even then they need the necessary nutrients and correct pruning to maintain good blooming.

Farmyard manure is an excellent addition to the soil in late winter or early spring; it needs two months or so to get into the ground. 'Never dig a rose bed' is what we are told, for the simple reason they are shallow rooted, and the hairy roots should not be broken. They need forking over carefully to merely incorporate the manure.

Fish blood and bone is something which could encourage rose sawfly, a problem which became evident after its use in this garden a few years ago, probably caused by the blood. The roses will need the addition of trace elements, bonemeal for strong roots and potash for the good flowers, which can be supplied by rock potash, wood ash occasionally or comfrey, mulched between the plants. The best form of trace element is seaweed meal. This will also take time to become active, so again give it a month or two to digest thoroughly. Roses always do well with the addition of magnesium, which may be necessary on light soils. A few ounces of Kieserite per plant will soon correct the problem.

NEMATODE (1mm) $\frac{1}{25}$"
Considered microscopic. Some cause damage to plants but others feed on bacteria and generally help, especially those which kill slugs.

If nitrogen is needed it can be added in the form of hoof and horn, but it is not recommended to overuse it, in order to prevent soft, sappy growth becoming a problem, which in turn encourages all manner of pests! French marigold, *Tagetes patula,* is a good addition to surround a rose bed as it is a help to kill off antagonistic nematodes which may be present. Old rose beds especially, soon become infested. Roses also favour as a companion plants such as Mignonette and Lupin, which also increase soil nitrogen and attract earthworms. An occasional foliar feed of liquid seaweed in early summer will also work as an extra deterrent to aphids by generally strengthening the roses' resistance.

PRUNING

These days pruning is becoming less obligatory, with some saying they do not bother. On the poorer soils plants are best pruned lightly and on better soil pruning can be a bit more drastic. However, it should be done for a reason; it enhances the buds and encourages growth, sometimes having a rejuvenating effect on a badly neglected rose. But as a yearly practice (March and April) its main purpose is to keep the rose healthy, allowing good freedom of air to pass through the blooms. If a rose suffers from mildew, the mildew should be pruned off, a good example being the rose *R. Frencham* (1946), which has a good scarlet colour and is very vigorous but suffers badly from mildew, usually on tender growth tips, so it is quite easy to prune off. Otherwise it is a good healthy rose.

Ramblers are pruned in the autumn with the main object of removing all flowered wood and replacing with the new growth, according to the season and amount of growth. Pruning climbers should be done according to the vigour of the plant. Very strong growing roses will become too thick and congested if left alone; they need the oldest growth removed and new growth introduced. Side shoots can be cut off to four buds or so, but should be left according to the space to be filled.

The less vigorous climbers like *R. Bantry Bay* will merely need dead wood removing. But use good discretion to fill in the empty spaces. Another rose in the same category is the *Rosa banksiae* which blooms on the sub laterals. But it will need pruning after a year or two, when great care should be taken to remove branches but not shoots – merely a thinning operation.

Old-fashioned shrub roses will not need regular pruning, perhaps once in three years to remove dead wood and older material. Dead-heading is the general policy, and the latest idea is to remove only a few inches of stem, when blooms will be produced much quicker.

7

Disease Control Predators

Building up a healthy garden also relies on plenty of favourable insects, which will do all the work for you if you have enough of them. Some years provide more insects than others, and cold summers are unlikely to encourage many of these sun loving little creatures. This is where biology has its influence in the garden. Just recently it was necessary for me to examine a Victoria plum for aphids. There were far too many, so it was essential to prune off all young growth to which they were attracted. But last year the problem was not even evident on this same tree as there were plenty of chalcid bugs which totally overwhelmed the green aphids; so, having performed the same examination, I allowed nature to get on with it!

The Americans have many sources to obtain predators of almost any description. During the past few years we have also been able to buy lacewings, plus a box to breed them in.

Several species for the greenhouse are available to deal with red spider mite (*phytosieulius*), vine weevil (*Nemasys H*), and mealy bug (*cryptolaemus*), none of which are cheap but most practical in a heated greenhouse.

In 1917 biological control was tried concerning a very troublesome Australian St Johns wort (hypericum) with a view to eradicating it by using insects (leaf beetles and some geometric moths). The insects taken from English hypericums were unsuccessful under Australian conditions, but a further import from France using a root-boring buprestrid beetle and a leaf beetle (*Chrysomela gemellata*) has become well established.

In New Zealand in the seventies they were troubled with some imported pest plants blackberry, gorse and ragwort. To tackle the gorse they introduced the seed-weevil (*Apion ulicis*) from England. The weevil has become well established and infests a high percentage of plant pods.

More trials with ragwort ended up using the ragwort seed-fly whose larvae live in developing florets and devour young seeds. The insect is now well established and is said to destroy nearly all the seeds in a floret.

PLANTING FOR PREDATORS

The design of the organic garden needs to allow for encouraging predators. If it is naturally wet with a stream running through it or has a pond there should be no trouble in encouraging frogs and toads, which will be a great help in dealing with slugs and snails.

Hedges can be chosen to include berrying kinds of plants for birds – cotoneasters, pyracantha, bird cherry; (*Prunus padus*), aronia, thorn, crataegas, berberis, viburnum, lonicera, ivy, holly, etc. There are one or two shrubs of Compositae and Umbelliferae families of interest, though most of these are on the tender side, the following work well for me – Ozothamnus (needs shelter), *Olearia hastii*; *Bupleurum fruticosum*; senecio, mostly on the smaller side;

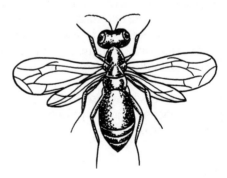

CHALCID WASP
⅛" (3mm long)
Has blue or green
metallic sheen on
its body. *Encarsia
Formosa* is of this family, used as a
biological control of whitefly in greenhouses

Chalcid wasp (×20)

45

mutisia; climbing gazania would be nice on a south wall and santolinas are most useful. In America they rate *Euonymus japonica* evergreen very highly as an 'insectary plant', giving it no less than ten insects including lacewings, chalcids and braconids. Also much complimented is oleander; this is of course a glasshouse plant, though it is new to me if it encourages anything else much but mealy bugs. However, *Euonymus* is more encouraging, making an excellent hedge. *Ruscus aculeatus* (butcher's broom) and *Choisya ternata*, both being evergreen, attract many ladybugs during their hibernation in winter. Other important insect attractants include alfalfa; angelica; buckwheat; carrot (*Daucus carota*); rue and amaranthus retroflexus (pigweed). The tree of heaven (*Ailanthus altissima*), which reaches 70 feet and is a native of Western China, is fast growing; apparently lives under a false name (tree of heaven rightly belongs only to *Ailanthus moluccana* because its branches, according to the people of the East Indies, reach towards paradise). The name was apparently transferred in the 1750s to the species *Ailanthus altissima* on its introduction to England; this tree, however, is most successful against atmospheric pollution and likes lighter soil without much moisture, also attracts at least five predators.

In the perennial border it is best to avoid bare patches especially in hot weather when predators could easily scorch. Good ground cover plants could include strawberry (*fragaria visca*), woodruff (*Asperula*), and various anthemis, geranium and cotoneaster spp; these encourage carabid and rove beetles.

Sedum spectabile is also a most useful late-flowering cover plant. Angelica (archangel), hollyhock (*Alcea rosea*) and willowherb (*Epilobium*) are recommended as a preferred environment for parasitic ichneumon wasps; these are of course among the best predators but regretfully all too rare. Also recommended as a good environment for lacewings are cinquefoil (*Potentilla*) and coreopis spp).

INSECTS

A quick look at Britain's greatest sources of predators shows there should be no shortage of potential. The largest group of all are the beetles, the largest order of animals in the world with over 300,000 species. Many of these species are of course pests, but it is fair to say the great majority are most beneficial to the positive growth of plants. Beetles can be aquatic or wood lovers, some live in fungi, flowers or leaves, many are good flyers. Stag beetles are now very rare and sightings are eagerly being recorded, often in oakwoods, sandy beaches, in towns and beneath logs and stumps, the latter being also a most common hiding place for both carabid and rove beetles. It is a good idea to leave some logs (approx 12") in various places to encourage beetles into the garden.

Soldier beetles are common on flowers and shrubs and nearly always with us, regardless of fickle weather, which seems to dictate to others such as the ladybirds, which are far less numerous in cool summers.

Not all of this vast family of beetles are useful predators. We also have pollen beetles, which hide inside flower heads and feed on pollen; fortunately they produce only one generation per year, and do move off to attack other pollen elsewhere, especially if encouraged by a hose of water on runner beans.

Lily beetles usually confine themselves to the lily flower and can easily be picked off. Leaf-eating beetles usually attack an unhealthy plant, but if a seaweed spray is used it tends to toughen up the foliage of the plant, so providing good resistance!

Since the early fifties there has been a noticeable decline in insect life in Warwickshire, for instance; as much as 20 per cent since records began in 1904. Mr George MacGavin, who has recently been in charge of an insect survey, has stated that 'insects are at the centre of ecosystems – take them away and everything else collapses.' Chris O'Toole, head of bee systematics at Oxford University, says that 'A quarter of Britain's 267 bee species are now endangered. Every third mouthful of our food is directly dependent on the unmanaged pollination services of bees. Without bees whole ecosystems will collapse and we are seeing that now!'

The organic system is solely reliant upon insects. One of the main contributors is the lacewing with 60 species in Britain. There are green and brown lacewings which feed on aphids, scale insects, mealy bugs and mites.

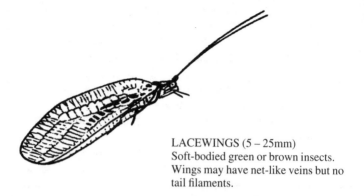

LACEWINGS (5 – 25mm)
Soft-bodied green or brown insects.
Wings may have net-like veins but no
tail filaments.

Perhaps the most startling insect to view is the ichneumon with its long abdomen and long ovipositor protruding from the end of its body. There are 2,000 species in Britain, and almost all are parasites on other insects. They can consume much more amounts of aphid population than the valuable hover fly. Ichneumons are now used in the glasshouse. Species (*Aphidius colemani*) are of the

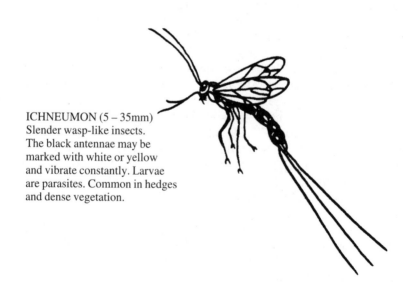

ICHNEUMON (5 – 35mm)
Slender wasp-like insects.
The black antennae may be
marked with white or yellow
and vibrate constantly. Larvae
are parasites. Common in hedges
and dense vegetation.

same family. They are most sensitive to insecticides, as are antho-corid bugs, which are so useful on fruit trees, eating aphids, cap-sids, scale insects, red spider mites and small caterpillars and black-kneed capsids, who also feed on red spider mites and live in trees.

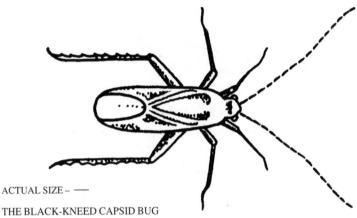

ACTUAL SIZE – ——

THE BLACK-KNEED CAPSID BUG
A vivid green body (females are a yellow green with paler eyes).
Black knees, dark red eyes and nymphs are almost yellow.

It was interesting to note that in my first organic garden for the first year or two raspberries were prone to the raspberry beetles so needed a regular derris spray. Also peas become maggoty if not sprayed in flower. It is many years since spraying for raspberries has been necessary and peas are most healthy, especially in their younger stages – older pods sometimes get an odd maggot but nothing to moan about. This of course is not a coincidence but the building up of natural defences, the balance of nature at work, encouraged by the right herbs, plants and environment.

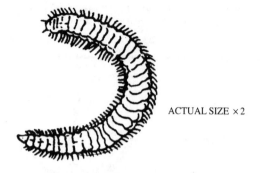

ACTUAL SIZE × 2

MILLIPEDE

Control with traps of potatoes or carrots in a tin pierced with holes.
Ducks and birds also enjoy them after digging, as do frogs and beetles!

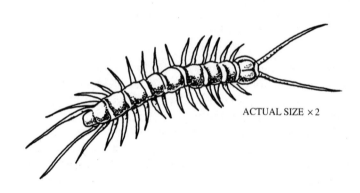

ACTUAL SIZE × 2

CENTIPEDES are friendly

Farmyard manure, forked around brassicas to prevent cabbage root fly

Lawn Spiker, 5" spikes, 1½ gall water used for ballast. Can be disassembled for transport

Lavender hedge. Lavender Farm, Heacham, Norfolk

Cerise Bouquet 12' x 12'

Seagull 25' x 15', M. Hambro's garden

Alternative to bonfires *Rotting Prunings*

Carabid Beetle

Hover Fly

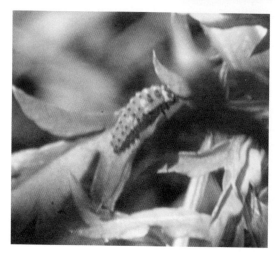

Lady Beetle Larvae

Mustard - Greenmanure - *Smothers*

Plum Tomatoes, *San Marzano* - Comfry Fed

Peach leaf Curl prevention, with plastic cover

Clematis, Delphinium, Hosta border. M. Hambro's garden

Sculptured Yew Hedge. Audley End

Euphorbia Mellifera, author's garden

Author standing next to compost bins

Anthemis tinctoria 'E C Buxton' and *Catananche caerulea 'Stargazer'* in the author's garden

Photo courtesy of Anne Green-Armytage

8

Move to Harpenden

The opportunity arose in the autumn of 1982 to take a head gardener's position at the Hyde, with Mr Hambro of the London banking family, so having successfully made my interview previously (complete with my curriculum vitae), we arrived at the Garden House an hour after the two-ton truck carrying all my worldly possessions had unloaded. We were about to make ready for a meal only to find that the cooker had no flex. However, Mr Hambro most kindly came to the rescue and we were able to fix the cooker, but not until 8 p.m. On the next day I met Bert and Ann, both members of the team of workers. Bert was quite instrumental in my being there at all, as he now only worked in the mornings. Having had a good gardening education as a journeyman with the Rothschild family, he knew his greenhouse work better than me and was relied upon for good sound judgement. He was quite a character and never missed an hour's television watching before coming to work, keeping us up to date with the latest news!

Ann was a student hoping to do landscaping as a career. She had a dark complexion and pigtails and had quite a gift for selecting the greenhouse jobs for most of the day.

Potting up arum lilies was my first job – about 20 with some spare for the garden outside and some for the Garden Cottage – the cottage was all on its own at a corner of the walled-in garden, which consisted of some two acres. The cottage garden was overgrown but had three gleditsia trees, two larix conifers, hydrangeas, a rhododendron, and two *Nyssa sylvatica* trees. The walled garden had some very nice plants in it amongst a lot of neglect, its centre-piece being rose beds forming a square, with lawn in between, with climbing roses Albertine, Dr Van Fleet and Alberic Barbier. A hedge in the garden consisted of *Stransvesia davidii fructo lutea* with both pink and yellow berries now known as photinia; these are fast-growing evergreens and reach tree height quite quickly if given the right conditions. Also within the walled garden was a long border beside a path which consisted of *Clematis jackmanii* at its rear, designed to fall over wire hoops to the front of the border whilst in between were clumps of delphiniums and at the front were *Hosta fortunii*. It had become immersed in bindweed (both *polygonum* and *convolvulus*) plus a good deal of ground elder. This was conquered in two or three weeks.

Outside the walled-in garden the main house had a beautiful cedar tree at the front overhanging the drive, which was precisely one mile long and also partly used by the 400-acre farm and part of the estate. The meadow around the drive frequently had Shetland ponies, which were tethered, until they occasionally broke loose and ran amok. It was our responsibility to collect them up when we noticed! Also living around the drive in the woods were muntjac deer, known as barking deer. They were very agile and could leap across the drive in front of a car in seconds.

My first problem came from inside the walled garden, where rabbits had made a way through and were enjoying the garden pinks amongst other delicacies. Shooting had not made a significant difference and so the best alternative was a cat. Mr Hambro would look for one as they only had a half dozen dogs. One morning Mr Hambro appeared walking up the path with a ginger and white moggy who, judging by the blood on Mr Hambro's arms, was not very friendly. However, he was introduced to my kitchen and a saucer of milk and became more friendly as time went on; in fact, after a week or two he was quite capable of leaping the garden wall and presenting me with half-grown rabbits on the doormat! My mother also had a nice little white cat which contributed to the good cause of clearing the rabbits from the garden, at which the pair of them worked brilliantly.

HEDGES

In front of the big house was a yew hedge which for some unknown reason had been allowed to 'rise' in the middle and looked anything but straight.

One or two things need to be borne in mind when hedging; one is that if you omit to cut it in the same place each year, it grows just a bit more than it should. The other one is to keep the 'flow' of the hedge as even as possible. A hedge is only as good as it looks from the outside, so it matters not if you have left a hollow in the middle which is not seen from the outside. Without going further into topiary, the secret of a good hedge is that it has to be wider at the bottom than the top, never more necessary than with a typical *Lonicera nitidum* hedge which will split in the middle if not correctly shaped.

Recently *Cupressus leylandii* has been highly criticized and has now come under parliamentary scrutiny, which is all for the best. It is of course a tree of great potential and can reach 100ft (30m) in Britain but can easily be restricted to 9ft (3m) or so, as a hedge, with a yearly trimming.

Having given some consideration to fast growing hedges/windbreaks, for preference the broom family is most suitable, especially for the light soil we have here. *Cytisus nigricans*, for instance is evergreen and flowers at least twice per year. *Cytisus scoparius* can reach 9ft (3m) and can be trimmed back gently; having a fairly short lifespan it can be planted in conjunction with a more permanent shrub hedge which will then take over and also benefit from the added nitrogen which this legume type of hedge produces.

Fastest Growing Hedge

Probably the fastest-growing hedge obtainable for privacy and a windbreak, evergreen or deciduous, can easily be produced from climbers, using a simple growing structure on which they can climb, the easiest being made of posts and wire e.g. 4ft × 6ft (1.2m × 1.8m) posts erected at 6–8ft

(1.8m–2.4m) intervals with strong wire in between, upward and crossing.

Russian vine (*Fallopia baldschuanica*) is unbeatable for speed of growth and becomes dense enough all year round for privacy. It is resistant to honey fungus, which was a necessity for my own situation in creating a hedge some years ago.

TREES AND SHRUBS WITH A LIMITED RESISTANCE TO HONEY FUNGUS

Ash	*Fraxinus excelsior*
Bamboos	*Arundinaria* and other genera
Barberry	*Berberis spp.*
Beech	*Fagus sylvatica*
Blackthorn (sloe)	*Prunus spinosa*
Box	*Buxus sempervirens*
*Box elder	*Acer negundo*
*Californian black walnut	*Juglans hindsii*
Cherry laurel	*Prunus laurocerasus*
Clematis	*Clematis spp.*
Douglas fir	*Pseudotsuga menziesii*
Elder	*Sambucus nigra*
Elaeagnus	*Elaeagnus spp.*
False acacia (Locust tree)	*Robinia pseudoacacia*
Fir (European, Grand, Noble)	*Abies alba, A. grandis, A. procera*
Hawthorn	*Crataegus spp.*
*Holly	*Ilex aquifolium*
Honeysuckle	*Lonicera nitida, L. periclymenum*
Incense cedar	*Calocedrus decurrens*
Ivy	*Hedera helix*
Junipers	*Juniperus*
Larch	*Larix spp.*
Mahonia	*Mahonia aquifolium, M. japonica*
Rock rose	*Cistus spp.*
Russian vine	*Polygonum baldschuanicum*
Smoke tree	*Rhus cotinus*
Stag's-horn sumach	*Rhus typhina*
Sweet chestnut	*Castanea sativa*

Sweet gum	*Liquidambar styraciflua*
Tamarisk	*Tamarix gallica*
Tree of heaven	*Ailanthus altissima*
*Yew	Taxus baccata

*Indicates virtually immune

GRASSES

Any herbaceous perennial or vegetable, provided these do not have starchy roots or tubers.

Clematis montana is most useful, a strong grower, varying in colour, white, pink, bronze, purple, in its different varieties. Other species may be suitable. Three are honeysuckles – especially *Lonicera japonica*; the evergreen *L. Halliana* is most useful for birds to rest in; the fragrant *L. henryi* is also evergreen with yellow flowers in June and July. Ivy (*Hedera*), though not perhaps a rapid climber in its early years, certainly will be when established; its variegated forms can be most attractive, e.g. *Hedera helix* Eva; H. helix Buttercup. Many ivies are shade tolerant.
Also among the fastest growing hedges are the pyracanthas;

PYRACANTHA

Pyracanthas – are most useful shrubs being evergreen and producing berries in autumn.

P. Angustifolia – is 3m (10ft) both in height and width. White flowers in early summer followed by yellow fruit. Frost hardy, –5°C (23°F).

P. Atalantiodes – 5m (15ft) H × 4m, (12ft) W. White flowers in summer followed by red fruit. Frost hardy.

P. Coccinea – 4m (12ft) both in height and width. Clusters of small white flowers, followed by bright red fruit. Fully hardy.

P. Mohave – 2.4m (8ft) × 23.4m, (8ft) White flowers produced in Corymbs, followed by long-lasting red berries deservedly popular due to its disease resistance to both fireblight and scab; frost hardy, –5C (23°F).

P. Orange Glow – Has received R.H.S. Garden Award of Merit, 3m (10ft) × 2.4m (8ft), glossy dark green leaves; small white flowers are produced in late spring, followed by a profusion of persistent orange-red to dark orange berries. Fully hardy and resistant to scab.

P. Shawnee – 3m × 4m (10ft × 12ft). A spreading shrub with narrowly elliptic, glossy, dark green leaves 5cm, (2in) long. Small white flowers in early summer followed by slightly flattened orange-yellow berries. Resistant to fireblight and scab; frost hardy, –5°C, (23°F).

My latest ideas with hedges, especially for smaller gardens and those needing a bit more colour, is using mainly evergreens and shrubs with good flowering or berrying capacity. Escallonia can be white, red or rose pink. Some varieties are more hardy than others; the white *E. Harold Comber* is very hardy, as is the apple-blossom pink *E. Slieve Donard*. Osmanthus decorative spring-flowering *Osmanthus burkwoodii* are very good evergreens. For fast growing evergreens there are also *Eucalyptus gunnii*, which grows up to two metres per year (very good for flower arrangers!); *Eleagnus ebbingei*, *Viburnum tinus*, and *V. burkwoodii*. These can easily be combined with deciduous shrubs if preferred, to complement the hedge/windbreak. Roses are a good choice and can be included in the hedge, especially those with Heps Moyesii varieties or rugosas, and good climbers.

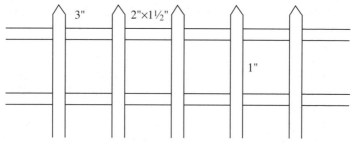

Simple support for strong climbers. Uprights close together. 3 inch posts 6 feet apart with three uprights in between. An organic wood preserver is recommended.

For the most reliable plain hedge, yew is always best. Common ivy is usually bad news for hedges, but it still can make a most useful evergreen and an especially good home for wrens, and its berries are a bonus. It is probably best to allow it to climb on a strong trellis or scaffold selected for it, where it remains harmless to other plants. Privet is too uneconomical in a smaller garden as it rapidly takes over all the surrounding area. The RSPB recommend the following shrubs for the best berries to feed birds.

SHRUBS THAT PROVIDE FOOD FOR BIRDS

Hawthorn	Honeysuckle	Japanese quince
Cotoneaster	Elder	Dogwood
Holly	Guelder rose	Privet
Snowberry	Barberry	Cherries
Climbing roses	Wayfaring tree	Yew
Buckthorn	Spindle	Crab apple
Ivy	Rowan	Firethorn

Any of these shrubs/trees can complement the garden hedge.

The gardener's cottage at the Hyde was situated outside the walled garden, the view on one side was quite stunning as it overlooked a valley to the main railway line to London. And beyond was the beautiful Luton Hoo house and garden, which on rising gave one quite an inspiration to begin the day. The cottage was adjacent to an apple orchard which had been choicely planted with such trees as Annie Elizabeth, a culinary very long keeper from December to June, and King of Pippins, a desert creamy yellow, juicy with a slightly bitter flavour but with 18 mg of vitamin C. Other varieties were School Master, Warners King, Allens Everlasting and Beauty of Kent. There were one or two common varieties, but a most interesting selection in all.

APPLES

Some apples contain more vitamin C than others. Amongst the cookers, Ontario* has been good for me, having 20 mg per 100 grams vitamin C. It is a large pale yellow apple $2\frac{3}{4} \times 2$ inches irregular. It is crisp and juicy and does not shrivel over a long period of keeping; discovered in America, keeps until April, and has frost-resistant blossom. Amongst other apples we have is the Wyken Pippin, which originated from Holland in 1720. This is a lovely little eater, greenish-yellow; the flesh is tender, yellow, aromatic, the eye, open, in a wide, shallow basin. Very welcome around Christmas time and keeps until January–February. We also have Woolbrook Russet, a cooker, with large green and russet fruit. It is rich in vitamin C and resistant to scab. It was rather slow to fruit well, but after a few years has steadily improved and is now healthier than it ever was.

The following apples are self-fertile.

ANNIE ELIZABETH a cooker, keeps well from September–April $3 \times 2\frac{3}{4}$ inches, oblong, conical irregular. Pale yellow, flushed and striped brilliant red. Flesh crisp, white, acid. Eye closed in a rather broad and deep basin. Origin Leicester 1868. Thoroughly commendable.

ADAM'S PEARMAIN good vitamin C 16.30 mg.

GREENSLEEVES (mid season), frost-free.

LORD LAMBOURNE an eater

REV. W. WILKS 1910, culinary, September–November, very large $3\frac{1}{2} \times 3$ inches flat conical, slightly irregular. Eye closed or slightly open, in a wide ribbed basin.

SUNSET (long keeper).

ALLINGTON PIPPIN 1906, dessert, $2\frac{1}{2} \times 2\frac{1}{2}$ inches, lemon yellow, slight red flush and faint stripes. Flesh is crisp, juicy, pale yellow, sub acid, aromatic.

WINSTON. This is also an apple we inherited, a lovely little apple aromatic $2\frac{1}{2} \times 2\frac{1}{2}$ inches conical, flesh red striped on yellow, either dessert or culinary, long keeper, March–April. It is a healthy tree and mostly free of scab.

Disease resistance

Apples showing a good measure of disease resistance
include Bountiful, Gala, Grenadier, Pixie, Redsleaves,
Sunset. Scab-prone trees can be aided by the addition of
chives planted around their trunks.

Recommended scab-resistant varieties:

American Mother
Ashmeads Kernel
Belle de Boskoop
Bramley Seedling
Charles Ross
Discovery
Egremont Russet
Ellison Orange*
Fortune

Grenadier
Kidds Orange Red
Red Devil
Red Ellison
Red Melba
Sparton
Sunset
Wagener*
Winston

*Frost Resistant Blossom

The largest apple of all appears to be Peasgood Nonsuch, a
culinary measuring $3\frac{3}{4} \times 2\frac{1}{2}$ inches, round flattened, irregular. Golden yellow with faint flush and a few broad broken
stripes. Flesh, tender, yellowish, pleasant flavour and cooks
frothily. Eye nearly closed in a deep round, even basin.
Raised by Mrs Peasgood of Stamford, 1858. Beautiful fruit.
Tree is rather prone to canker. Peasgood Nonsuch is also the
parent of Rev. W. Wilks with Ribston. The latter, an excellent
dessert pippin which has the biggest vitamin C content of
30.6mg, is a great favourite. It was raised at Ribston Hall,
Knaresborough, about 1709, from seeds brought from
Rouen. Medium to large apple $3 \times 2\frac{1}{2}$ inches round conical,
irregular. Yellow with dull brownish-red flush and a few
stripes and russet. Flesh is firm, yellow, highly aromatic. Eye
a little open, in a deep uneven basin.

Pruning

It is important to know which trees are which, especially
with regard to pruning, the most tricky situation if it is not

known if the tree is a tip bearer or not! Trees which bear fruit at the end of a branch and on its laterals, which should not be removed should merely be thinned from year to year.

ANTHOCORIS NEMORUM BUG

Colour dark red brown,
related to the Water Boatman
'Beetle'.

– ACTUAL SIZE

Trees of this description are as follows:

Ellisons Orange

Exeter Cross

George Cave

Irish Peach

Worcester Pearmain*

Bismarck

Gladstone

Laxtons Superb

Lady Sudeley

St Edmunds Russet

Winston

Cornish Gilliflower

*Frost Resistant Blossom
(Bramley Seedling is partially a tip bearer and needs 'lengthy' laterals and sub laterals or these can be left as tip bearers.)

There are several different methods of pruning. Some varieties bear fruit on 'short' laterals e.g. Cox's Orange Pippin types, Sturmer, Rev. Wilks.

Other varieties, such as Blenheim Orange, Beauty of Bath, and Allington Pippin, bear fruit on 'longer' laterals. (Shorter laterals are three or four buds and the longer laterals five or six buds, pruned in winter, preferably in the new year, February being the best month.)

Other detailed pruning methods known as 'Courtois' or

'Lorette' systems involve summer pruning similar to the pruning necessary with wall-trained fruit, cordon or espalier-trained trees.

General pruning needs to be done to avoid the tree overcrowding its branches; the tree should have an open centre with branches fanning out from the middle, which can be shortened by one third. Laterals or side shoots should not be closer than 6 inches (15cm) apart and shortened by a half or less; these form spur systems, which need thinning each year.

Pears have similar pruning requirements to apples, so can be treated in a similar fashion. Mildew sometimes attacks the fruit blossom, often proving fatal. A good remedy is to spray urine with three parts water over the tree in February or March.

On Sunday we often took the opportunity to attend a service at Flamstead Church, a beautiful little church in a very tasteful little village with a most welcoming congregation. Amongst them was a working priest, Rev. George King, who divided his time between the church and the nearby Rothamstead agricultural experimental station, where some most interesting experiments have been made. The most renowned concerned the Broadbalk wheat field, which has grown wheat every year since 1843 and is given 14 tons per acre of farmyard manure per year. One of its plots has had no manure of any sort since 1839. The soils of the two plots have been tested for nitrogen each year; the unmanured plot still had 0.105% in 1945 whilst the manured plot had 0.236%.

SOIL AND ITS FOOD

At Rothamstead much work has been taken up on the structure of humus, but very little has been discovered. As it does not form crystals, neither X-ray photography nor the electron microscope has revealed much, and standard chemical methods have given little information. But 40–60% of humus is an acid called humic acid, which is combined with calcium as a soil base. Both the acid and the calcium can be divided up using a dilute alkali and dilute

hydrochloric acid respectively. Little is known about the con-
stituents of soil organic matter, but taken as a whole, nitrogen is
split up in the form of 25–30% protein, 5–10% amino sugars and
40–50% as yet unidentified. Usually more than half the surface
soil consists of half organic phosphorus.

Clay minerals play a most important part in maintaining proteins and important amino compounds from being dislodged and
oxidized by soil organisms. The proteins rapidly decompose into
ammonia and then into nitrates. Nitrates are quickly washed out
by rain but the protection by clay colloids ensures that at least 1%
of total soil nitrogen is available in any one growing season.

Certainly humus is a most complex and difficult mystery of the
soil; it is active in its water holding capacity, it is the product of
dead matter, vegetable and animal waste and all that makes for
good compost.

One could sum up and say that humus is the perfect ingredient
of the soil, the result of much activity from worms, animals,
insects, innumerable different kinds of bacteria and fungi, and
needs to be replaced continually.

The discovery of the marvels of the soil and the necessity for
healthy plant growth is the main difference between the organic
grower and the chemical grower, who is only concerned with an
immediate result or quick return from his investment.

We enter into a new world when delving into the soil, the basis
of organic growing. Most important are earthworms; they can
virtually turn over the soil and eliminate digging altogether. Three
million worms, as discovered by Darwin, can produce an extra ton
per acre of soil. Numbers can be deceiving; one worm produces
600 worms in a year, and Dr Shewell Cooper says that he counted
12 million per acre or 30 million per hectare. Soil produced by
worm-casts has five to ten times more nutrients than average soil.
They are a hub of activity, encouraging bacteria which produce at
a rate of 16 million in 24 hours and are common to most soils.
Rhizobium and azotobacter are both bacteria and produce growth
regulators called gibberellins. These are taken up by the plant to
stimulate early growth of tomatoes and boost the swelling of
potatoes. They are found in good organic soils.

Both bacteria and fungi produce antibiotics; 300 have been

identified but there are believed to be 1,000 more as yet unidentified. Streptomycin is active against many micro-organisms causing spots, blight, wilts and rots. Griseofulvin is produced by bacteria and is effective against powdery mildew, rusts and botrytis.

One gram of soil contains 3,000 million bacteria, which is rather difficult to imagine but gives us an idea of the vast life abounding in the soil.

Nematodes are tiny wormlike organisms and one of the most common life forms of the soil. They produce eggs and are encouraged by the stimulation of plant roots. They remain around plant roots from birth onwards and parasitise and consume many organisms, including bacteria, earthworms, snails, fungi, beetles, slugs, algae and aphids. They are generally good for the garden and can be used most successfully as a biological control of slugs.

The latest use of nematodes is in the product known as Nemasys H, consisting of naturally occurring microscopic nematodes which seek out vine weevil larvae. It is mixed with water and used with a watering can in the soil 12°C or above (May–June) and early autumn (September) (from The Organic Catalogue, HDRA). This is a good step forward. My previous prevention against vine weevils (not always easy to get) is soot, used around plants. Vine weevils are most attracted to peat composts.

Mycorrhizae

'Myco' means fungal and 'rhiza' means root. Mycelia invade a plant's roots; they live partly in soil and partly in the root. Mycorrhizae take carbohydrates from the root and in return give nitrogen.

Mycorrhizae are dependent on compost and plant activity in the soil and account for the many benefits of keeping the soil well covered in winter with a green manure or mulch to ensure that they are not washed out by winter rains. They are totally discouraged or even inhibited by the use of chemical fertilizers containing nitrogen as this will weaken their potential to resist disease, a point very clearly explained by the late Sir Albert Howard:

The long-continued use of artificials is followed by disease and the production of indifferent fruit. The strawberry is a mycorrhiza former and those who grow strawberries can very easily compare the effect of humus and chemical fertilisers on the health of the plants and on the quality of the fruit. The mycorrhiza appear to be the machinery provided by nature for the fungi living on the humus in the soil to transmit direct to the active areas of roots, the contents of their own cells. If as seems almost certain growth-promoting substances (roughly corresponding to vitamins in food), it would be necessary to get these into the plant undamaged and with the least possible delay. The mycorrhizal association in the roots, by which a rapid and protective passage for such substances is provided, seems to be one of nature's ways of helping the plant to resist disease.

No Dig

No digging ensures fertility in the top few inches of the soil, where plants begin their life, and will continue to find nourishment, provided by mulches and composts. Mulches and fertility are conserved by green manures in winter, and therefore mycorrhizae are also preserved. Digging can often bury compost deeper than the roots of a plant, often eliminating it after only one year. For growing runner beans and Brussels sprouts it is a good policy to trench them, ensuring plenty of fertility for gross feeders. Brussels sprouts need deep friable soil, and well-rotted manure or compost, so trenching would suit them well, or just plain forking. No digging also saves time, so valued in springtime when more important jobs are to be done. Many weed seeds lie dormant in the earth for many years and only need a little light to chick them. Better to leave them in the dark where they can remain without digging them up.

One common problem for organic gardeners is the fact of producing lots of worms, which in turn provide food for moles. My policy with these is to use most methods, my favourite is to grow *Euphorbia Lathyris*–Moleplant in their vicinity, which works for roughly four months of the year (June–September), when the plants can reach 6 feet (1.8 metres) quite easily; with repulsive roots to match, these are objectionable to our little friend the mole. The procedure should be to plant the euphorbias in main runs along the places of entry to the garden. (Euphorbias have the unique position of being the only plant to produce boron, that most useful mineral so essential to root crops such as celery.) Moles also dislike soot; when preparing a seedbed in spring, before seeding rake in a little soot. Soot has 4% Nitrogen but should be used only in small quantities as it can burn. An old method used to some effect was to flatten the mole run, then proceed to open up the mole hill, fill it with water, then pour a little oil on the surface of the water; as the water descends, so does the oil floating on its surface, and coming into contact with the mole, shortly effects its destruction – by blocking its breathing tubes. It works best on lawns! Using elder leaves buried in the mole run is also said to send off moles, who find the smell most offensive.

9

Green Manures

There are about 14 different green manures (not including that most useful little annual *Limnanthus douglasii*, which attracts hoverflies and remains in the garden in a thick mass all the winter). They can be split into those most useful for heavy or light land.

My land is light/sandy and so it is best to use mustard, tares, phacelia, trefoil and rye. The reason is that they are most suited for overwintering after most crops have gone. Green manure needs to be bulky, with good germination. Then we can decide either to compost it, dig it in or leave it. Mustard grows quickly, can be sown in September and smothers weeds better than any other except possibly rye. It will remain until cut off by cold weather with little remaining in the spring except a good clean soil on which to sow. The other outstanding one is tares or vetches, which can also be sown up to September but is a nitrogen fixer with NPK. It overwinters and is prolific, making excellent manure to lightly dig in or to compost and mulch later. Rye is most useful as it can wait until October to be sown, and is very bulky, rooty and hardy. Phacelia is almost unique in that it is a Compositae and therefore a good predator attractant; after its use as a manure it produces its pretty blue flowers. Field beans are a good alternative, being nitrogen fixers, also suitable for heavier soil, as are the flowers which on some soils give only patchy germination. Lupins are not prolific on this soil but are also nitrogen fixers; buckwheat is not prolific here but is most useful as a predator for hoverflies; it is also good to bring in pheasants and as a source of calcium.

Fenugreek is perhaps the most unusual, being a good medicinal herb which also has culinary uses in Indian dishes, in curry powder, pickles etc. It is hardy and a nitrogen fixer, most useful for quick summer use and for bulky material. Lucerne or alfalfa – hardy, suitable for dry, light, well drained soil – is used as a herb and eaten in moderation, but not for rheumatoid arthritis sufferers. It can be cut up to five times per year for manure, silage etc.

After digging in, the green manure should be allowed to settle for one month at least before sowing seeds, to avoid the release of various compounds. This can be even more important if turf has been dug in, and can prove disastrous if planted before rotting down. Kent wild white clover is excellent for the lawn, and is also used between rows of vegetables as a suppressor.

COMPOST – latest ideas

Over a period of the last five years a new era of composting has begun, after much research and experimentation; the Centre of Alternative Technology at Machynlleth, Powys, Wales, recommends several alternatives to the original ideas. Why alter the system? Well! Britain lags way behind when it comes to recycling. We manage to recycle only 8% of household waste, whilst such countries as Switzerland, Norway and Sweden already recycle 50%; and countries such as Denmark, Germany, or Canada and America already manage 30%.

The other significant reason is to make composting easier and more practical to understand, for the average gardener and householder.

Broadly speaking, the emphasis now is on air flow in the heap, more moisture to encourage rotting, and the encouragement of nature, allowing visible invertebrate decomposers, brandling worms, woodlice, slugs, insect larvae, springtails and mites, plus carnivores such as centipedes and staphylinid beetles. There is no need for turning the compost. But the emphasis is also on water, or rather its adjustment, so that the compost is not too wet or too dry.

Structure of bins

Recommended sizes of compost bins are based on the original size of 3ft × 3ft (1m × 1m) square. The idea (see diagram) shows three bins linked together with the purpose of using the largest with rough material, twiggy cuttings, even sods of grass, leaves and weeds of all descriptions, tough perennials, stems etc. The bin is 6ft (1.8m) high and will take at least a year to produce well-rotted compost, whilst the two attached bins can be used for fresh material in the process of making and completed compost ready for use.

Shredded material will always make the best compost and will often be from prunings which are carbon and help to bulk up the whole, contrasting well with the other essential ingredients such as lawn mowings and other more nitrogenous products. As a bin is built up, to encourage the air flow good use can be made of toilet-roll spindles, scrunched up cereal boxes, used tissues, kitchen towels or soiled newspapers generally mixed together in equal proportions with all the other material.

Perhaps it is worth mentioning that tinfoil, bottle tops, oasis, plastic, spoons and forks do not compost even after one year!

Experiment has proved that totally covering the compost bin is a mistake, so to eliminate adding water, it is preferable to half cover the bin, so allowing extra moisture to penetrate through the mixture more evenly. Then cover the completed compost as is usual, until it is used.

My experience with vermin is that they will only penetrate the bin from underneath and that rats are capable of ruining the whole heap. The most practical 'bottom' for the bin is a produce called Gridweld or weldmesh used in protecting machinery by agricultural engineers, which should last for years and allow worms and soil agents to enter the compost.

Plastic bags are most useful for containing seeding weeds, waste potatoes, large quantities of twitch or elder, left to rot down and used for trenching or added to rough compost.

Autumn leaves can be collected in them and used in the same way but should be provided with holes, for good leaf mould. Or more normally a leaf container can be made with wire netting, one

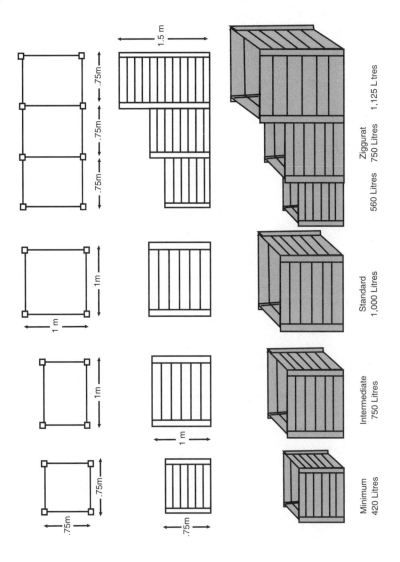

.75m .75m | 1 m | 1 m | .75m .75m .75m

.75m | 1 m | 1 m | .75m

1.5 m

Minimum
420 Litres

Intermediate
750 Litres

Standard
1,000 Litres

560 Litres   750 Litres   Ziggurat   1,125 Litres

69

measuring 6ft × 3ft × 4ft (1.8m × 0.9m × 1.2m) will hold enough leaves for an average garden of ten trees and at least a dozen shrubs of medium size.

High mineral composting materials

The combination of plants and kitchen waste can either make or mar the composition of the finished product. The following herbs all contain NPK (nitrogen, phosphate, potash) as well as other minerals:

FAT HEN – *Chenopodium album*, a former vegetable, also contains calcium, iron and sulphur.

PURSLANE – *Portulaca oleracea*, contains calcium, used as a salad or cooked vegetable.

YARROW – *Achillea mollis*, contains copper, magnesium. A Compositae plant, and activator.

VETCH – *Tares vicia sativa*. A nitrogen fixer, green manure, copper and cobalt.

NETTLE – *Urtica dioica*, activator, vitamins A & C, minerals and iron.

COMFREY – *Symphytum uplandicum*, activator, calcium, manganese, cobalt, silicon, iron.

Other plants of particular note:

BRACKEN – *Pterium aquilinum* in its green state 2% nitrogen, 3% potassium, also iron, copper, manganese, cobalt.

DANDELION – *Taraxacum vulgare*, officinale sodium, silicon, manganese, calcium, potassium, iron, copper, nitrogen.

FERTILIZERS

Gardening on light soil demands frequent attention to the feeding of plants; they can lack in minerals very quickly, especially magnesium and lime; this is rectified best by using *dolomite*, probably the best form of lime, which lasts a year or two longer, then ground lime.

Calcified seaweed – contains 50% lime, plus magnesium and many trace elements.

Fish, blood and bone – a most useful form of nitrogen and phosphate; but very often contains oxide chemicals. It can be used in conjunction with comfrey to make a well balanced fertilizer but can be replaced by using *hoof & horn*: bone meal and wood ash, 13% nitrogen, 22% phosphate, 8–10% K.

Fish Meal – why is it not possible to buy an organic form? Said to be perfect for growing asparagus. We have to be content with a liquid form. It is 5–10% nitrogen, 5–10% phosphate, plus trace elements.

Kieserite – a naturally occurring mineral high in magnesium (16%), a good replacement for Epsom salts.

Gypsum – A claybreaker with calcium and sulphur. Could prove valuable for the necessary calcium on lawns.

Seaweed Meal – has by far the most trace elements of any fertilizer; can be used as an activator for compost. Has nitrogen and potash and a small amount of phosphate, rock phosphate 26%, rock potash 10.5%.

Chilean nitrate of potash – a traditional fertilizer with nitrogen and potassium. Produced from natural deposits. Together with rock, a natural fertilizer and a good source of minerals, especially favoured by vegetarian growers who prefer not to use fertilizers derived from animal resources. Rock potash 10.5%, rock phosphate 27%.

FERTILIZER REQUIREMENT TABLE

Non manure	Proportions			Sandy/	Heavy well
	N	P	K	Poor soil*	manured
Bean Broad	6.0	25	25	100g (3oz)	50g (1½oz) sq yd
Bean French	15	25	27	180g (5oz)	90g (2½oz)
Beetroot (6.2–6.6PH)	25	10	30	210g (6oz)	140g (4oz)
Cabbage Spring	30	20	30	210g (6oz)	100g (3oz)
Carrot	6.0	25	25	35g (1oz)	0
Celery + (Boron)	9	2	5		
Leek	9.0	30	27	210g (6oz)	100g (3oz)
Onion	9.0	30	27.5	180g (5oz)	90g (2½oz)

Parsnips	10	17.5	22.5	35g (1oz)	0
Spinach/leaf Beet				280g (8oz)	140g (4oz)
Sweet Corn	15	15	15	140g (4oz)	70g (2oz)
Turnips/Swede + Boron	7	15	15	70g (2oz)	35g (1oz)

Manure/Compost

Bean Runner	15	25	27	180g (5oz)	100g (3oz)
Blackcurrant	7.5	11	25		
Broccoli Sprouting	7.1	17	30	210g (6oz)	100g (3oz)
Brussels sprouts	25	17.5	20	350g (10oz)	180g (5oz)
Cabbage	30	20	30	350g (10oz)	180g (5oz)
Calabrese	7	17	30	210g (6oz)	100g (3oz)
Cauliflower	7.5	17.5	30	280g (8oz)	140g (4oz)
Courgette/marrow	10	20	25	210g (6oz)	100g (3oz)
Gooseberries	7	7	7		
Lettuce				180g (5oz)	90g (2½oz)
Pea	0	7.5	12	0	0
Potato, early				210g (6oz)	100g (3oz)
Potato, maincrop	15	15	20	280g (8oz)	140g (4oz)
Tomato	10	20	25	140g (4oz)	70g (2oz)
Tomato, outdoor	10	20	25		
Strawberries	0	11	22		
Raspberries	7.5	11	25		

Organic Fertilisers

Bone Meal	3.5	20.0	–	4oz sq yd	(120gm/sq m)
Fish meal	9	7	–	3oz sq yd	(85gm/sq m)
Dried Blood	9	1	–	2–4 oz sq yd	(60–120gm/sq m)
Rock Potash	–	–	10	8oz sq yd	(225 gm/sq m)
Potash (Chase & Cumulus)	–	–	13–20	High Value!	
Rock Phos	–	27	–	8oz sq yd	(225 gm/sq m)
Blood Fish & Bone	4.5	7	–	4–6oz sq yd	(120–18 gm/sq m)

Compound Balanced Organic Fertilisers

Hoof & Horn	12–14%			150 gms pellets	per sq m
+ Bone + potash (rock)					
Processed chicken manure	5	3.4	2.8	200 gms	per sq m
Offal, manure, Cocoa					
Shells fermentation					
product	6	6	6	70–140gms	per sq m
Shellfish Waste	3.5	2	3	200–300 gms	per sq m
Mealworm manure	3	3	3	35–100 powder	per sq m

* requirements per sq yd (based on 7%N)

10

Euphorbias

When we moved to West Norfolk to this light, stony soil plus several dry summers, we needed to find plants suitable for those conditions; without building up humus it is virtually a question of starting at square one. The obvious solution came to me after my first purchase of a *Euphorbia wulfenii*, which seemed to fit this situation perfectly without too much need of any fertilizer (though they prefer some compost).

Euphorbias can virtually flower at all times of the year, some preferring shade, but most of them are happy in the sun. *Euphorbia wulfenii* and *Euphorbia characais* are very similar but found in different parts of the world, though different in height, *Wulferii* being taller and yellowish as opposed to the reddish brown or purplish black of *characais*. These two subspecies now have at least 27 variations or cultivars between them, which is more than most.

For continual flowering perhaps the best and longest must be *E. ceratocarpa*, which makes a good show at the rear of the border (4ft – 1.2 m). *E. dulcis* rates highly, giving a show in spring followed by shades of red in the autumn. *E. polychroma*, yellow-green, also welcomes in spring, with *E. myrsinites* (9 ins – 22.5cm) which is good on a wall or rockery. *E. Griffithii* is a nice apricot red, spreading mainly from its roots, it prefers moisture (3ft H: – 0.9m). One of my favourites is *E. robbiae* flowering from spring to summer and very useful in shade, yellow-green colour (18ft – 45cm). *E. corallioides* (2ft – 0.6m) yellow, is best treated as an annual as it appears to be short-lived, but seeds very prolifically each year, flowering all summer.

73

Euphorbias are notoriously known to be hard to identify. There is great confusion between *E. caroloides*, *E. wallichii*, and *E. longifolia*, though *E. longifolia* is later flowering. Other forms are much more identifiable. *E. cyparissias* can spread unbelievably fast, with its feathery foliage, though flowering over several months, covering soil by rootlets, so effective ground cover. *E. cyparissias* Purple Tip is a good improvement on the ordinary form. *E. nicaeensis* (8 ins–2ft – 20–60 cm high), very effective and makes a good show; my latest is *E. nicaeensis* from Hungary, and very prolific, flowering longer than its parent. *E. martinii* is a good euphorbia with red-tinged shoots, flowering from spring to mid-summer; it produces terminal cymes, 3–4 ins (9cm–10cm) across, yellow-green cyathia with dark red nectar glands. (3ft – 0.9m). It can suffer from mildew if it is not in an open position.

Perhaps the most famous of all at Christmas time is *Euphorbia pulcherrima* – Poinsettia – available in white as well as the deep reds and pinks. They are long lasting plants and reward for careful attention; needing 65–70°F in winter. After flowering, it is possible to cut back foliage to 6 ins (2cm), resting until May, when the growing season starts, until November, then they need a short day treatment for eight weeks with 10 or 14 hours' darkness. But if they are kept in very shady conditions for at least one month, they can be induced to flower at any time of the year.

Many other euphorbias are tender and only suitable for conservatories. The euphorbia species total 10,000. The white juice which exudes from plants is poisonous and also an irritant if allowed to touch sensitive areas of the body.

BIBLIOGRAPHY

Gardening from Which, 2 Maryleborne Road, London NW1 4DX

The Companion Planting Chart, Michael Littlewood FLI; FSGD. Higher Hayne, Somerset

Grow Your Own Fruit & Vegetables, Hills, L.D., Faber

The World of the Soil, Russell, Sir John, Collins

Insects, Letts Pocket Guide to, Forey, Pamela & Fitzsimons, Cecilia

Soil Humus & Health, Shewell-Cooper, Dr W.E., Good Gardeners Association

The Gardener's Guide to Common-Sense Pest Control, Olkowski, William, Door, Sheila, Olkowski, Helga, The Taunton Press

Comfrey Sympho Symphytum, Clarke, Philip, The Pentland Press

Fertility Gardening, Hills, Lawrence D., HDRA

A Guide to Habitat Creation, Baines, Chris & Smart, Jane, Packard Publishing Ltd

The New Rose Expert, Hessayon, Dr D.G., Expert Books, Transworld

Garden Predators (leaflet) Hadlow College

The New Perennial Garden, Kingsbury, Noel, Frances Lincoln Ltd

The Amateur's Greenhouse, Sanders, T.W., FLS, FRHS (1904) WH&L Collingridge

GRASS SEED HOUSES

Andrews, Anthony D, Bourne, Lincolnshire
Barenbrug UK Ltd. Bury St Edmunds, Suffolk
Boughton Loam Ltd, Kettering, Northamptonshire
Collier Turf Care Distributors Ltd, King's Lynn, Norfolk
Down to Earth Landscapes Ltd, Colchester, Essex
Nickersons Force Limagrain, Rothwell, Market Rasen, Lincoln-
    shire
Links Turf Layers (UK), Carstor, Lincolnshire
Nickerson Zwaan, Market Rasen, Lincolnshire
Nursery Supplies (Bourne) Ltd, Bourne, Lincolnshire
Sovereign Turf Ltd, Norwich
Boughton Loam Ltd, Kettering, Northamptonshire
British Wild Flower Plants, Great Yarmouth, Norfolk
Mommersteeg, Sleaford, Lincolnshire
Cotswold Grass Seeds Direct. The Barn Business Centre, Gt
    Rissington, Cheltenham Glos.
Perryfield ProRange, Perryfield Holdings, Thorn Farm,
    Lukberrow, Worcs

INDEX